Street Atlas of
PLYMOU

C000216063

Key to Maps

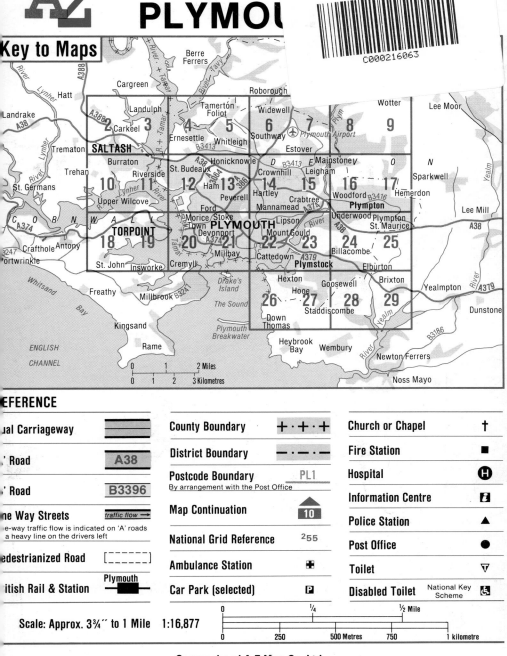

Scale: 0 1 2 Miles / 0 1 2 3 Kilometres

REFERENCE

ual Carriageway		County Boundary	+ · + · +	Church or Chapel	†
' Road	A38	District Boundary	— · — · —	Fire Station	■
' Road	B3396	Postcode Boundary	PL1	Hospital	⊞
		By arrangement with the Post Office			
ne Way Streets	traffic flow →	Map Continuation	▲ 10	Information Centre	ⓘ
e-way traffic flow is indicated on 'A' roads a heavy line on the drivers left		National Grid Reference	255	Police Station	▲
edestrianized Road	[- - - - -]			Post Office	●
		Ambulance Station	✚	Toilet	▽
itish Rail & Station	Plymouth ■	Car Park (selected)	▣	Disabled Toilet	National Key Scheme ♿

Scale: Approx. 3¾″ to 1 Mile 1:16,877

0   ¼   ½ Mile
0   250   500 Metres   750   1 kilometre

Geographers' A-Z Map Co. Ltd.

Head Office: Vestry Road, Sevenoaks, Kent TN14 5EP   Telephone 0732 451152
Showrooms: 44 Gray's Inn Road, Holborn, London WC1X 8LR   Telephone 071-242 9246

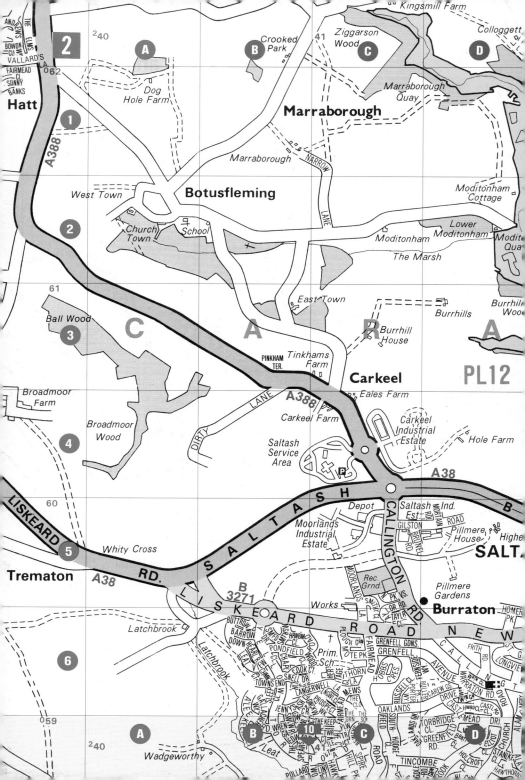

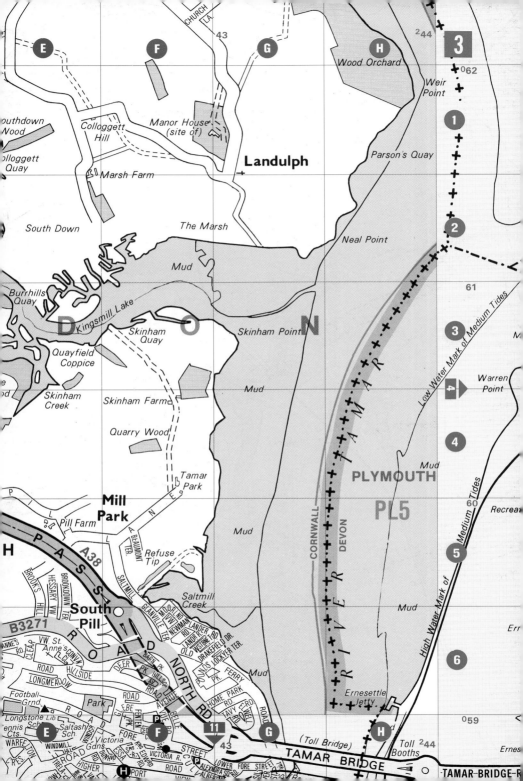

CHURCH LA.

43

3

244

062

E

F

G

H

Wood Orchard

Weir
Point

1

Southdown
Wood

Colloggett
Hill

Manor House
(site of)

Landulph

Parson's Quay

Colloggett
Quay

Marsh Farm

2

Marsh Farm

South Down

The Marsh

Neal Point

61

Mud

Skinham Point

3

Low Water Mark of Medium Tides

Burrhills
Quay

Kingsmill Lake

D

Skinham
Quay

O

N

Warren
Point

4

Quayfield
Coppice

Skinham Point

Mud

4

Skinham
Creek

Skinham Farm

Mud

Mud

PLYMOUTH

Quarry Wood

T
A
M
A
R

PL5

Tamar
Park

Mud

60

**Mill
Park**

P

Medium Tides

Recrea

I
L
L

Pill Farm

L

CORNWALL   DEVON

5

A38

Refuse
Tip

L
A
N
E

Mud

High Water Mark of

H

P
A
S
S
A
G
E

BROOKS HILL
HESSARY VW
BROOKDOWN TER

SALTMILL

Saltmill
Creek

R
I
V
E
R

Mud

6

South Pill

SALTMILL
GLANVILLE TER
WOOD LA
NEWMAN RD
LANDER RD
LANDRAKE RD
OLD WISTERN
DRAKEFIELD DR
NOS LOCKYER TER

Mud

B3271

ROAD

ST ANNE'S
CTS

NORTH RD

Ernesettle
Jetty

059

244

ANNE'S
RD
CLEAR
VW ST
ANNE'S RD

ROAD
HILLSIDE

DYER
PK
HILLS RD
BARN PK
FENTEN PK

HOME PARK
RD
DAVY FORD
WELL
FERRY
RD

Ernes

LONGMEADOW

ROAD

E

Longstone Lib
Tennis Sch

Football
Grnd.

Park

Saltash
Sch

F

BELLE VUE

G

(Toll Bridge)

Toll
Booths

H

WINDMILL
WARFE
CRES

Victoria
Gdns

FORE
STREET

11

43

Victoria R.
ALEXANDRA SQD
ALFRED

LOWER FORE STREET

TAMAR BRIDGE

TAMAR-BRIDGE-R

H

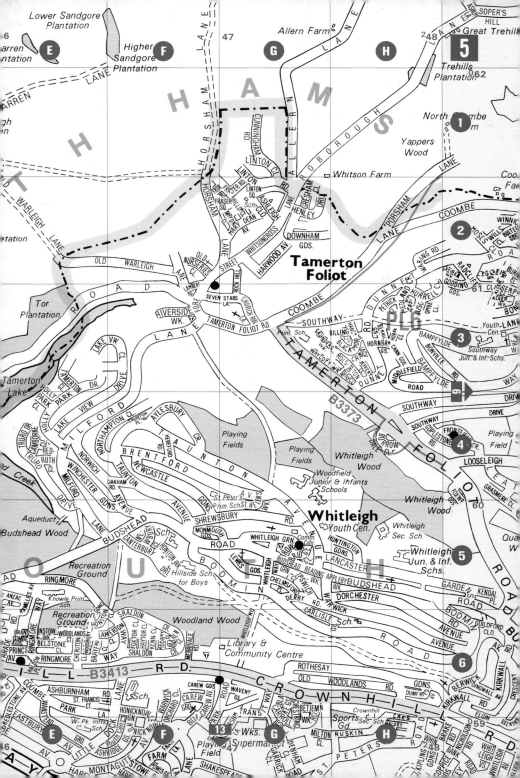

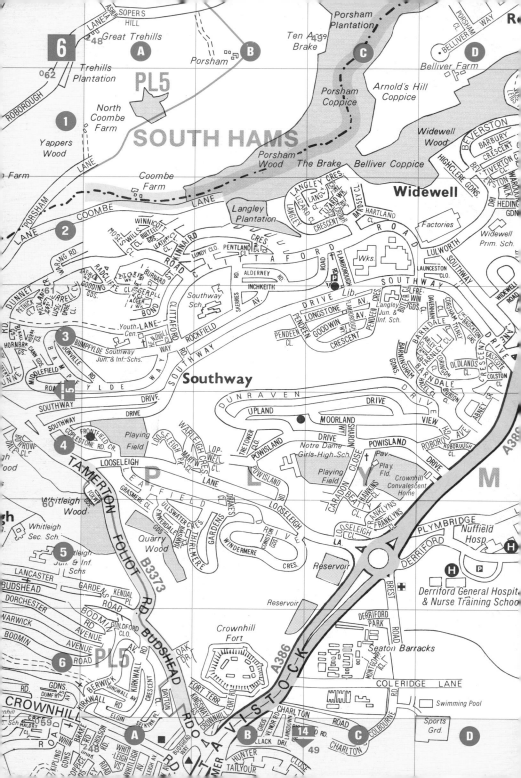

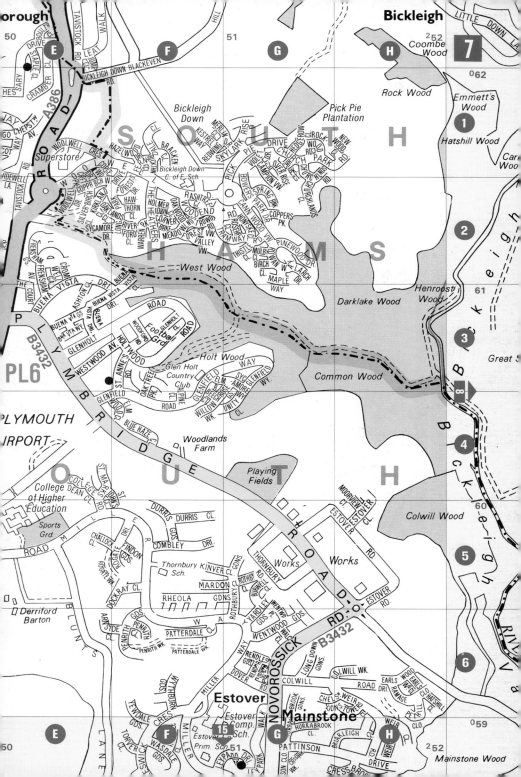

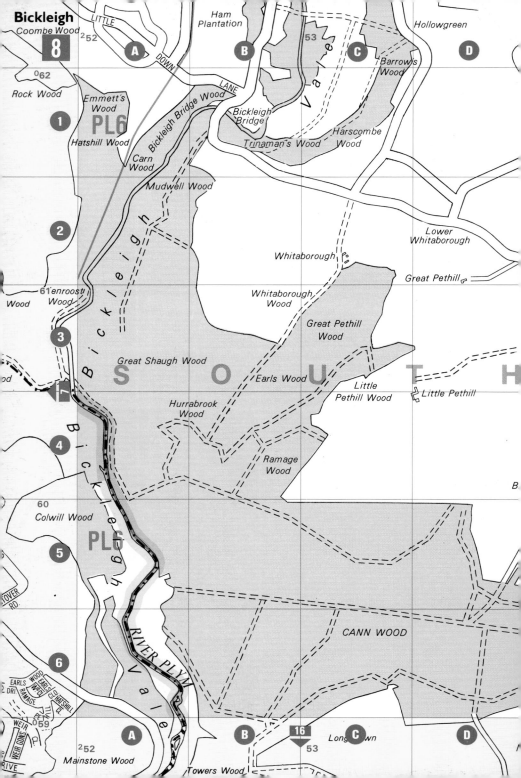

E
F
G
H

254
55
Collard Tor.
256
062

Bughill

Wotter

1

Faunstone

PORT LANE

COLLARD

China Clay
Works

2

Port
Lane
End

Coldstone
Farm

61

PL7

Browney
Cross

H A M S

Truelove

3

M

ton Barton

Portworthy

4

60

Boringdon
Camp

5

PARK LANE

Fernhill Wood

Heathdown
Cottage

Lower
Hooksbury
Wood

Bude Farm

6

Higher
Effordleigh

Coney Park
Plantation

Tory Brook

E
F
G
H

254ll's Farm

17

55

256

059

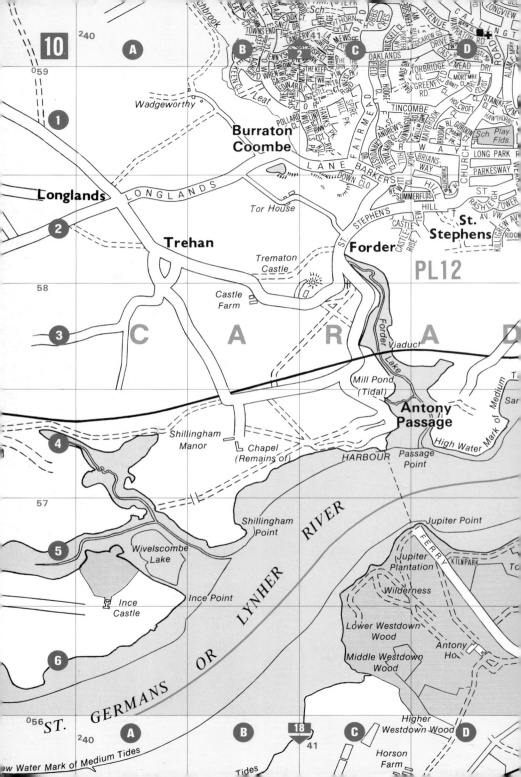

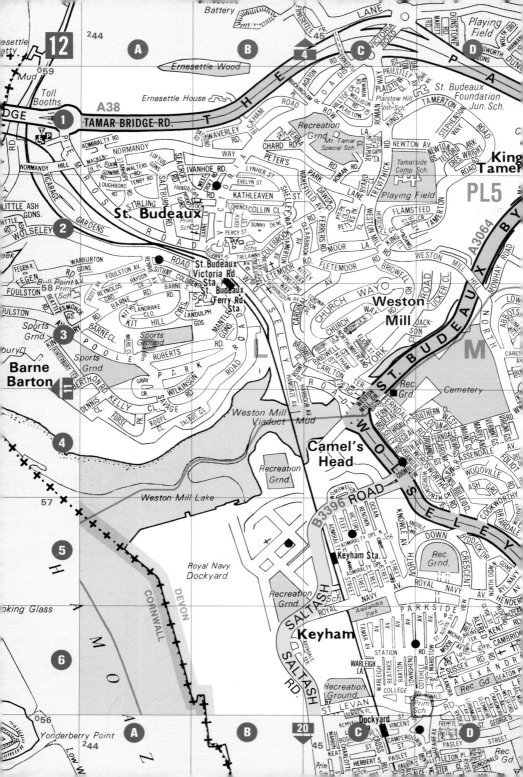

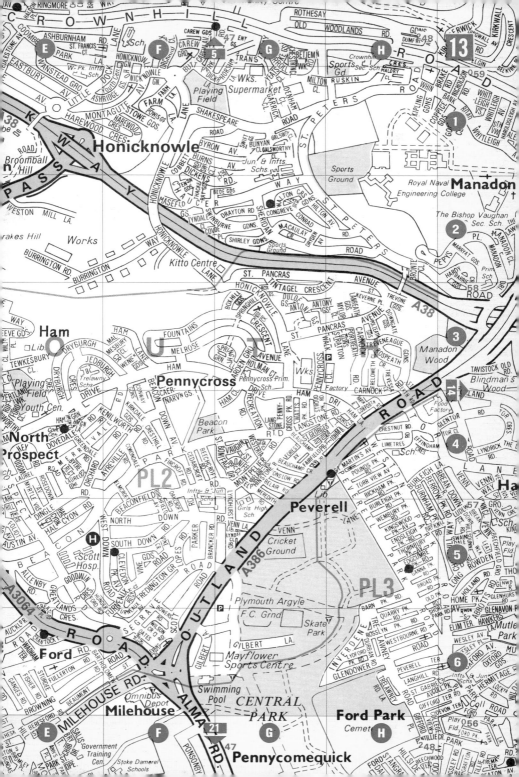

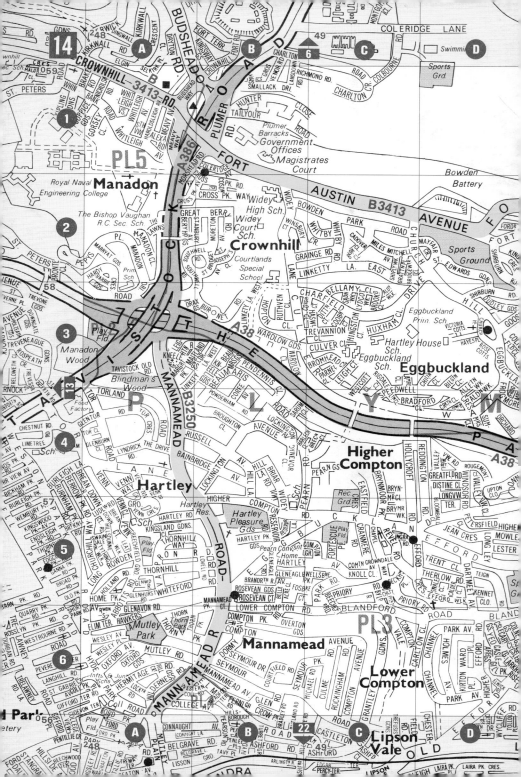

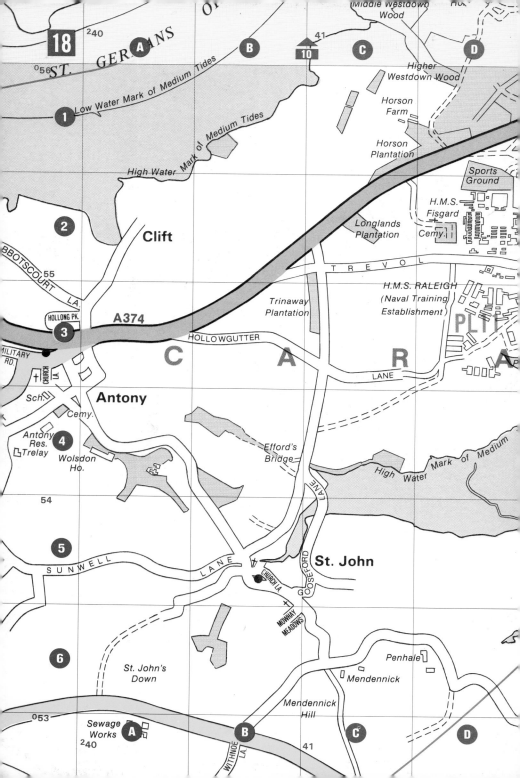

ST. GERMANS

⁰56

Low Water Mark of Medium Tides

High Water Mark of Medium Tides

Middle Westdown Wood

Higher Westdown Wood

Horson Farm

Horson Plantation

Longlands Plantation

Sports Ground

H.M.S. Fisgard Cemy.

Clift

ABBOTSCOURT LA.

55

HOLLONG PK.

A374

MILITARY RD.

HOLLOWGUTTER

TREVOL

H.M.S. RALEIGH
(Naval Training Establishment)

PLY

Trinaway Plantation

C   A   R   A

LANE

Church

Sch.

Antony

Cemy.

Antony Res.
Trelay

Wolsdon Ho.

Efford's Bridge

High Water Mark of Medium

54

SUNWELL

LANE

St. John

CHURCH LA.

GOOSEFORD LANE

MOWHAY MEADOWS

St. John's Down

Penhale

Mendennick

Mendennick Hill

⁰53

Sewage Works

²40

WITHNOE LA.

41

41

10

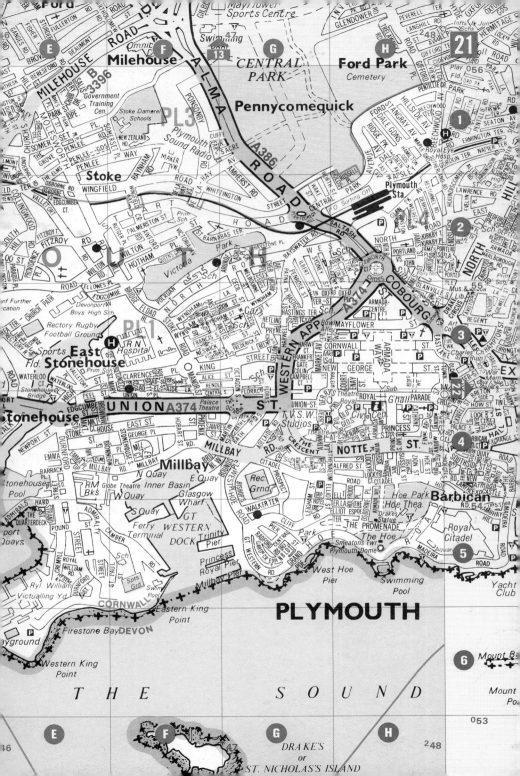

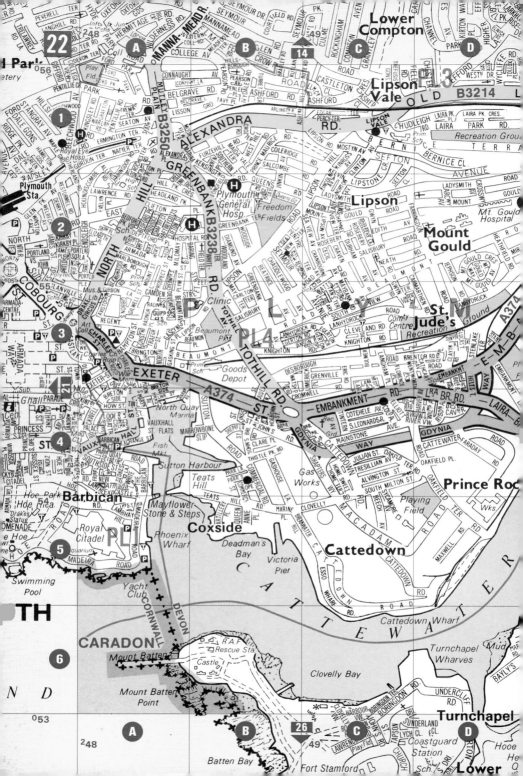

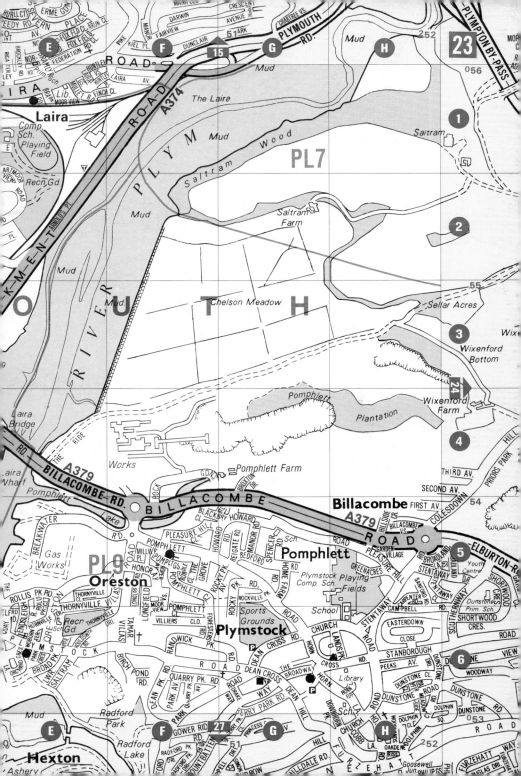

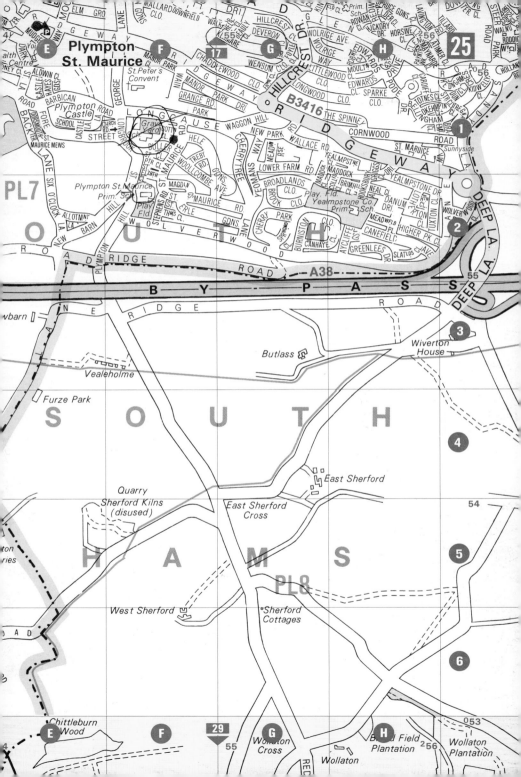

053

A **B** 22 **C** UNDERCO RD **D**

Mount Batten

Rescue Sta.

Castle

Clovelly Bay 49

Turnchape Wharves

BAYLY

Mount Batten Point

CLOVELLY RD

HARBUUR VW

BORINGDON TER

BORINGDON RD

UNDERLAND DRI

UNDERLAND CL.

Turnchape

BARTON

Hoo h.

1

Batten Bay

Fort Stamford Country Club

BORINGDON RD

NOSS JOHN'S RD

LAWRENCE RD

LYCH RD

Play Fld

ST. JOHN'S RD

CHURCH HILL

Coastguard Station

Sch

PYNE

Lower Hooe

Dunstone Point

Football Ground

STAMFORD CL

STAMFORD HILL

ST. JOHN'S DRI

RACHEL CL.

LAKE RD

HEXTO

YOND

2

Rum Bay

JENNYCLIFF LANE

WESTWAY

BELBRICK

POLLARD CL.

STEW CL.

BEARE RD

Sch

LE

Play Fld

BELLE VUE RISE

SEA VIEW AVE.

BELLE

HOE

P

West Hooe L

SHA SCOT. RD

DEVON

52

Jennycliff Bay

PL9

W. T. Station

3

Stadd

STADDON

4

Ramscliff Point

Rams Cliff

Staddon Heights

Golf Course

Brownhill Battery

Leekbed Bay

51

S O U T

5

Bovisand Pier

Staddon Point

Bovisand Cottage

B O V I

Caravan Park

Bovisand Lodge

Brim Copp

6

Bovisand Bay

Madam's Hill

050

²48

A **B** 49 **C** **D**

Crownhill Bay

Manor Bourne 5

MANOR

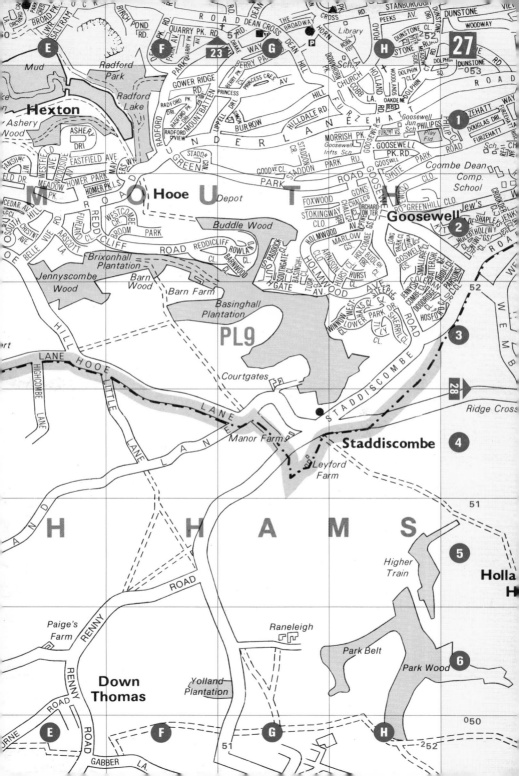

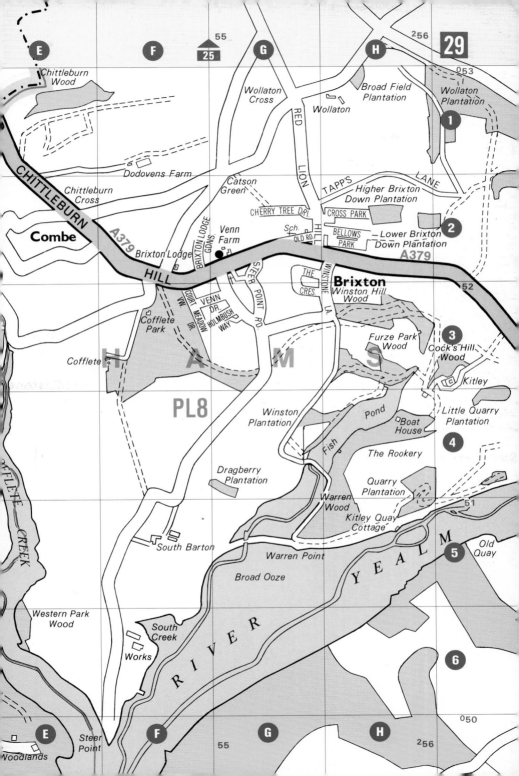

E

F

▲ 55
25

G

H

256

053

Chittleburn Wood

Wollaton Cross

Wollaton

Broad Field Plantation

Wollaton Plantation

1

RED LION

CHITTLEBURN

Dodovens Farm

Catson Green

Chittleburn Cross

Combe

A379

HILL

Brixton Lodge

CHERRY TREE DR.

BRIXTON LODGE GDNS.

Venn Farm

Sch.

OLD RD.

TAPP'S

CROSS PARK

BELLOWS PARK

Higher Brixton Down Plantation

LANE

Lower Brixton Down Plantation

2

A379

52

STEER POINT RD.

THE CRES.

WINSTONE LA.

Brixton

Winston Hill Wood

VW. DR.

COURT MEADOW DR.

VENN DR.

HOLMBUSH WAY

Cofflete Park

Cofflete

H   A   M   S

PL8

Winston Plantation

Dragberry Plantation

Furze Park Wood

Fish

Pond

Boat House

The Rookery

Cock's Hill Wood

3

Kitley

Little Quarry Plantation

4

Quarry Plantation

Warren Wood

Kitley Quay Cottage

51

South Barton

Warren Point

Broad Ooze

R   I   V   E   R   Y   E   A   L   M

5

Old Quay

6

Western Park Wood

South Creek

Works

Woodlands

E

Steer Point

F

55

G

H

256

050

PLACES OF INTEREST

Sketch Map - not to scale

A374
Ferry St.
Torpoint
River Tamar
Dockyards
Devonport
Vehicle Ferry
Ferry Rd.
A374
Saltash Road
Albert Road
Park Av.
Chapel Street
Fore Street
Devonport Station
Dockyard Station
A3064
A386
Mount Wise
Admirals Hard
Durnford Street
Millbay
Union Street
Stoke Rd.
Devonport Rd.
Milehouse Road
Passenger Ferry
Cremyll
Mount Edgcumbe House & Country Park
H.M.S. Plymouth
West Hoe Rd.
Cliff Rd.
Grand Pde.
Drake's Mem.
Plymouth Dome
The Hoe
Citadel Rd.
The Crescent
Theatre Royal
Civic Centre
Western Approach
R.C. Cathedral
North Rd. West
A374
A386
Saltash Rd.
Central Park
Mayflower Sports Centre
Drakes Island NT
The Sound
Swimming Pool Rd.
Smeaton's Tower
Hoe Road
Aquarium
Armada Mem.
Armada Experience
Guildhall
Royal Parade
Market
Car Park
Car Park
Shopping Centre
Coburg Street
Plymouth Station
Hyde Park Rd.
Mannamead Rd.
Mount Batten Point
Madeira Road
The Citadel
Phoenix Wharf (River Trips)
Barbican
Lambhay Hill
Elizabethan House
Merchant's House
New St.
Notte St.
Prysten House
St. Andrew's Church
Southside St.
Vauxhall St.
Mayflower Steps
Plymouth Gin Distillery
Mayflower Gin Distillery
Coach Station
Drake Cir.
Exeter Street
A374
Tothill Rd.
Greenbank Rd.
Museum & Art Gallery
Alexandra Rd.
Car Park
A379 Road

INDEX TO STREETS

HOW TO USE THIS INDEX

(a) A strict alphabetical order is followed in which Av., Rd., St., etc. are read in full and as part of the name preceding them; e.g. Adela Rd. follows Adelaide St. Ope but precedes Admirals Hard.
(b) Each street is followed by its Postal Code District Number and map reference; e.g. Abbey Pl. PL1—4H 21 is in the Plymouth 1 Postal Code District and is to be found in square 4H on page 21.

N.B. The Postal Code District Numbers given in this index are, in fact, only the first part of the Postcode to each address and are only meant to indicate the Postal Code District in which each street is situated.

ABBREVIATIONS USED IN THIS INDEX

All : Alley	Cir : Circus	Ga : Gate	Mkt : Market	Rd : Road
App : Approach	Clo : Close	Gt : Great	M : Mews	S : South
Arc : Arcade	Comn : Common	Grn : Green	Mt : Mount	Sq : Square
Av : Avenue	Cotts : Cottages	Gro : Grove	N : North	Sta : Station
Bk : Back	Ct : Court	Ho : House	Pal : Palace	St : Street
Boulevd : Boulevard	Cres : Crescent	Ind : Industrial	Pde : Parade	Ter : Terrace
Bri : Bridge	Dri : Drive	Junct : Junction	Pk : Park	Up : Upper
B'way : Broadway	E : East	La : Lane	Pas : Passage	Vs : Villas
Bldgs : Buildings	Embkmt : Embankment	Lit : Little	Pl : Place	Wlk : Walk
Chyd : Churchyard	Est : Estate	Lwr : Lower	PL : Plymouth	W : West
Circ : Circle	Gdns : Gardens	Mans : Mansions	Prom : Promenade	Yd : Yard

Abbey Pl. PL1—4H 21
Abbotsbury Way. PL2—3D 12
Abbotscourt La. PL11—3A 18
Abbotts Rd. PL3—6A 14
Abingdon Rd. PL4—1A 22
Abney Cres. PL6—4D 6
Acklington Pl. PL5—5C 4
Acre Cotts. PL1—2D 20
Acre Pl. PL1—2D 20
Adams Clo. PL5—2C 12
Adams Clo. PL11—2E 19
Adams Cres. PL11—2E 19
Addison Rd. PL4—2A 22
Adelaide La. PL1—4F 21
Adelaide Pl. PL1—3F 21
Adelaide Rd. PL1—4G 21
Adelaide St. PL1—3F 21
Adelaide St. PL1—6D 12
Adelaide St. Ope. PL1—3F 21
Adela Rd. PL11—2G 19
Admirals Hard. PL1—5E 21
Admiralty Ope N. PL2—5C 12
Admiralty Ope S. PL2—5C 12
Admiralty Rd. PL5—1A 8
Admiralty St. PL1—5E 21
Admiralty St. PL2—5C 12
Agaton Rd. PL5—1C 12
Ainslie Ter. PL2—4C 12
Aire Gdns. PL3—6D 14
Alamein Rd. PL12—1D 10
Albany St. PL1—3C 20
Albemarle Vs. PL1—2D 20
Albert Rd. PL2—2C 20
Albert Rd. PL12—1F 11
Albion Ct. PL11—2H 19
Albion Rd. PL11—2H 19
Alden Wlk. PL4—4D 14
Alderney Rd. PL6—2B 6
Aldersley Wlk. PL6—3C 14
Aldwin Clo. PL7—1E 25
Aldwin Rd. PL7—6G 17
Alee Rd. PL12—6B 2
Alexandra Clo. PL9—5B 24
Alexandra Pl. PL4—1A 22
Alexandra Rd. PL2—6D 12
Alexandra Rd. PL4—1A 22
Alexandra Rd. PL5—1A 14
Alexandra Sq. PL12—1F 11
Alexandra Ter. PL2—6D 12
Alfred Pl. PL2—6D 12

Alfred Rd. PL2—6D 12
Alfred St. PL1—4H 21
Alger Wlk. PL6—3A 6
Alicester Clo. PL2—1C 20
Alice St. PL1—3F 21
Allenby Rd. PL2—5E 13
Allendale Rd. PL4—1A 22
Allern La. PL5—1G 5
Allerton Wlk. PL6—4D 14
Alleyn Gdns. PL3—3A 14
Allotment La. PL7—2E 25
Alma St. PL4—4B 22
Almeria Ct. PL7—1C 24
Almond Dri. PL7—5H 17
Alpine Clo. PL6—3F 7
Alton Pl. PL4—1A 22
Alton Rd. PL4—1A 22
Alvington St. PL4—4C 22
Amacre Dri. PL9—1D 26
Amados Clo. PL7—1B 24
Amados Dri. PL7—1C 24
Amados Rise. PL7—1C 24
Amherst Rd. PL3—1G 21
Amity Pl. PL4—2A 22 -
Andrew's Way. PL12—1A 2
Andurn Clo. PL9—1B 28
Ann's Pl. PL3—1E 21
Anson Pl. PL2—1C 20
Anson Pl. PL4—3B 22
Anstis St. PL1—3F 21
(in two parts)
Antony Gdns. PL2—3G 13
Antony Rd. PL11—1G 19
Anzac Av. PL5—5E 5
Appleby Wlk. PL5—5G 5
Apsley Rd. PL4—1H 21
Arcadia. PL9—1D 28
Arcadia Rd. PL9—6C 24
Archer Pl. PL1—2G 21
Archer Ter. PL1—3G 21
Archway Av. PL4—2D 22
Arden Gro. PL2—3G 13
Arkham Clo. PL7—5C 16
Arkwright Gdns. PL5—1D 12
Arley Clo. PL6—3D 6
Arlington Rd. PL4—1B 22
Armada Centre. PL1—3H 21
Armada St. PL4—2A 22
Armada Way. PL1—3H 21
(in three parts)
Arnison Clo. PL9—2G 27

Arnold's Pl. PL4—2E 23
Arnside Clo. PL6—6E 7
Arscott La. PL9—2E 27
Arthur Ter. PL11—2H 19
Artillery Pl. PL4—5B 22
Arun Clo. PL3—6E 15
Arundel Cres. PL1—2G 21
Arundel Ter. PL2—1D 20
Ashburnham Rd. PL5—6E 5
Ash Clo. PL12—6B 2
Ashcombe Clo. PL7—4C 16
Ashdown Clo. PL6—6G 7
Ashdown Wlk. PL6—6G 7
Ashery Dri. PL9—1E 27
Ashford Clo. PL3—1C 22
Ashford Cres. PL3—1C 22
Ashford Hill. PL4—1B 22
Ashford Rd. PL4—1B 22
Ash Gro. PL2—4D 12
Ashleigh Clo. PL5—2G 5
Ashleigh La. PL5—1H 5
Ashley Pl. PL1—2G 21
Ashridge Gdns. PL5—1E 13
Ashton Clo. PL6—3E 7
Ashtree Clo. PL6—2F 7
Ashwood Clo. PL7—6H 17
Ashwood Pk. Rd. PL7—5H 17
Aspen Gdns. PL7—6H 17
Athenaeum La. PL1—4G 21
Athenaeum Pl. PL1—4G 21
Athenaeum St. PL1—4G 21
Atherton Pl. PL2—1C 20
Auckland Rd. PL2—6E 13
Austin Av. PL2—5E 13
Austin Cres. PL6—2E 15
Avent Wlk. PL7—4E 17
Avon Clo. PL3—5F 15
Avondale Ter. PL2—6C 12
Axe Clo. PL3—5F 15
Aycliff Gdns. PL7—2H 25
Aylesbury Cres. PL5—4F 5
Aylwin Clo. PL7—5E 17
Ayreville Rd. PL2—4E 13

Babbacombe Clo. PL6—3G 15
Babis Farm Clo. PL12—1F 11
Babis Farm Ct. PL12—2F 11
Babis Farm M. PL12—1E 11
Babis Farm Row. PL12—1F 11
Babis Farm Way. PL12—2F 11

Babis La. PL12—2F 11
Back Hill. PL12—1D 10
Back La. PL7—1E 25
Bainbridge Av. PL3—4A 14
Bainbridge Ct. PL7—4D 16
Bakers Clo. PL7—6H 17
Balfour Ter. PL2—1C 20
Balmoral Av. PL2—6D 12
Bampfylde Way. PL6—3H 5
Bampton Rd. PL6—2F 15
Barbican Ct. PL4—4A 22
Barbican Rd. PL7—1E 25
Barbican, The. PL1—4A 22
Barbury Cres. PL6—1D 6
Bardsey Clo. PL6—2C 6
Bargote Wlk. PL6—3E 15
Baring St. PL4—2A 22
Barker's Hill. PL12—1C 10
Barndale Cres. PL6—3C 6
Barne Clo. PL5—3A 12
Barne La. PL5—2B 12
Barne Rd. PL5—3A 12
Barn Field Dri. PL7—6H 17
Barningham Gdns. PL6—3C 6
Barn Pk. PL12—6F 3
Barn Pk. Rd. PL3—6H 13
Barnstaple Clo. PL6—3F 15
Barnwood Clo. PL9—2G 27
Barossa Rd. PL11—2H 19
Barrack Pl. PL1—4E 21
Barrie Gdns. PL5—2A 14
Barrow Down. PL12—6B 2
Bartholomew Rd. PL2—6E 13
Bartlett Wlk. PL7—6F 17
Barton Av. PL2—6C 12
Barton Clo. PL7—6H 17
Barton Rd. PL9—1D 26
Basinghall Clo. PL9—2G 27
Basket Ope. PL1—4A 22
Bath La. PL1—4G 21
Bath Pl. PL1—4G 21
Bath Pl. W. PL1—4G 21
Bath St. PL1—4G 21
Battershall Clo. PL9—2H 27
Battery La. PL4—4A 22
Battery St. PL1—3F 21
Baydon Clo. PL2—6E 15
Bayly's Rd. PL9—6D 22
Bayswater Rd. PL1—2G 21
Beacon Down Av. PL2—3F 13
Beaconfield Rd. PL2—5F 13

Beacon Pk. Rd. PL2—5E 13
Beare Clo. PL9—2D 26
Bearsdown Clo. PL6—3E 15
Bearsdown Rd. PL6—3D 14
Beatie Rd. PL5—3H 11
Beatrice Av. PL2—6C 12
Beatrice Av. PL4—2B 22
Beatrice Av. PL12—1E 11
Beatty Clo. PL6—4C 6
Beauchamp Cres. PL2—4G 13
Beauchamp Rd. PL2—4G 13
Beaudyn Wlk. PL6—4E 15
Beauly Clo. PL7—6G 17
Beaumaris Gdns. PL3—3B 14
Beaumaris Rd. PL3—3B 14
Beaumont Av. PL4—3A 22
Beaumont Pl. PL4—3A 22
Beaumont Rd. PL4—3A 22
Beaumont St. PL2—6E 13
Beaumont Ter. PL12—5F 3
Beckford Clo. PL7—6G 17
Beckham Pl. PL3—5C 14
Bede Gdns. PL5—2F 13
Bedford Pk. PL4—2A 22
Bedford Pk. Vs. PL4—2A 22
Bedford Rd. PL9—5G 23
Bedford St. PL2—5D 12
Bedford Ter. PL4—2A 22
Bedford Way. PL1—3H 21
Beech Av. PL4—5C 22
Beech Clo. PL11—2G 19
Beech Ct. PL6—4F 7
Beechcroft Rd. PL2—4F 13
Beechcroft Rd. PL3—5C 14
Beechfield Gro. PL3—5A 14
Beechwood Av. PL4—1H 21
Beechwood Rise. PL6—2G 15
Beechwood Ter. PL4—1H 21
Beeston Wlk. PL3—4E 15
Belair Rd. PL2—4G 13
Belair Vs. PL2—4G 13
Belgrave La. PL4—1A 22
Belgrave Rd. PL4—1A 22
Bellamy Clo. PL6—3C 14
Bell Clo. PL7—4F 17
Belle Acre Clo. PL3—5B 14
Belle Vue Av. PL9—2D 26
Belle Vue Dri. PL9—2D 26
Belle Vue Rise. PL9—2D 26
Belle Vue Rd. PL9—2E 27
Belle Vue Rd. PL12—1F 11

Bellingham Cres. PL7—1H 25
Belliver Way. PL6—1D 6
Bellows Pk. PL8—2H 29
Belmont Pl. PL3—1E 21
Belmont St. PL1—3G 21
Belmont Vs. PL3—1D 20
Belstone Clo. PL5—6E 5
Benbow St. PL2—1D 20
Bennett St. PL1—4C 20
Beresford St. PL2—1E 21
Bernice Clo. PL4—1D 22
Bernice Ter. PL4—1C 22
Berrow Pk. Rd. PL3—4H 13
Berry Head Gdns. PL6—2A 14
Berry Pk. Clo. PL9—1G 27
Berry Pk. Rd. PL9—6G 23
Berthon Rd. PL5—3A 12
Berwick Av. PL5—6A 6
Betjeman Wlk. PL5—6G 5
(in two parts)
Beverley Rd. PL3—1D 22
Beverston Way. PL6—1D 6
Beweys Pk. PL12—1C 10
Beyrout Pl. PL1—2D 20
Bickern Rd. PL11—2H 19
Bickham Pk. Rd. PL3—4H 13
Bickham Rd. PL5—1B 12
Bickleigh Clo. PL6—2C 14
Bickleigh Down Rd. PL6—1E 7
Bicton Clo. PL6—2G 7
Biddick Dri. PL2—5D 12
Bideford Wlk. PL6—3G 15
Bigbury Wlk. PL6—3G 15
Biggin Hill. PL5—5D 4
Bilbury St. PL4—3A 22
Billacombe Rd. PL9—4E 23
Billacombe Vs. PL9—5H 23
Billing Clo. PL6—3G 5
Billington Clo. PL6—3D 14
Birbeck Clo. PL7—4E 17
Bircham View. PL6—2E 15
Birch Clo. PL6—2G 7
Birchfield Av. PL2—4F 13
Birch Pond Rd. PL9—6F 23
Birchwood Gdns. PL7—4G 17
Birkdale Clo. PL12—1C 10
Bishop's Pl. PL1—4G 21
Blackall Gdns. PL6—3H 5
Blackberry Clo. PL9—5F 23
Blackberry La. PL9—5F 23
Blackeven Hill. PL6—1F 7
Blackfriars La. PL1—4A 22
Blackmore Cres. PL6—3H 5
Blackstone Clo. PL9—1B 28
Blackthorn Clo. PL6—1F 7
Blairgowrie Rd. PL5—1A 12
Blake Gdns. PL5—6G 5
Blanchard Pl. PL7—4E 17
Blandford Rd. PL3—5C 14
Blenheim Rd. PL4—2A 22
Bloomball Clo. PL3—5D 14
Blue Haze Clo. PL6—4F 7
Blunts La. PL6—5E 7
Bodmin Rd. PL5—5F 5
Bond St. PL6—3A 6
Bonville Rd. PL6—3H 5
Boon's Pl. PL1—2G 21
Boringdon Clo. PL7—4D 16
Boringdon Hill. PL7—3E 17
Boringdon Rd. PL7—5D 16
Boringdon Rd. PL12—1C 26
Boringdon Ter. PL9—6C 22
Boringdon Vs. PL7—5D 16
Borough Ct. PL11—1E 19
Borough La. PL11—1E 19
Borough Pk. PL11—1E 19
Borringdon Av. PL5—3B 12
Borrowdale Clo. PL6—4H 5
Boscastle Gdns. PL2—3G 13
Boscawen Pl. PL2—1C 20
Boswell Clo. PL5—1F 13
Bouldon Clo. PL7—6H 17
Boulter Clo. PL6—1E 7
Bounds Pl. PL1—4G 21
Bourne Clo. PL3—5F 15
Boville La. PL9—6B 24
Bovisand La. PL9—5D 26
Bowden Clo. PL12—1A 2

Bowden Pk. Rd. PL6—2B 14
Bowers Pk. Dri. PL6—2G 7
Bowers Rd. PL2—5F 13
Bowhays Wlk. PL6—4E 15
Boxhill Gdns. PL6—2G 13
Bracken Clo. PL6—1F 7
Braddons Hill. PL7—5B 16
Bradfield Clo. PL6—2G 15
Bradford Rd. PL6—4C 14
Bradley Rd. PL4—1B 22
Braemer Clo. PL7—1H 25
Brake Rd. PL5—1A 14
Bramble Wlk. PL6—4E 15
Bramfield Pl. PL6—4F 15
Bramley Rd. PL3—6E 15
Brandon Rd. PL3—1E 23
Brandreth Rd. PL3—5B 14
Branicker Rd. PL2—5F 13
Branscombe Gdns. PL6—6E 5
Bransons Ct. PL7—6H 17
Braunton Wlk. PL6—3G 15
Brayford Clo. PL5—6E 5
Breakwater Hill. PL4—5B 22
Breakwater Rd. PL9—5E 23
Brean Down Clo. PL3—5A 14
Brean Down Rd. PL3—4H 13
Brecon Clo. PL3—4C 14
Brentford Av. PL5—4F 5
Brent Knoll Rd. PL3—5H 13
Brentor Rd. PL4—3C 22
Brest Rd. PL6—5C 6
Breton Side. PL4—4A 22
Brett Wlk. PL7—4F 17
Briansway. PL12—1D 10
Briardale Rd. PL2—5D 12
Briarleigh Clo. PL6—1G 15
Briar Rd. PL3—4B 14
Bridges, The. PL12—2E 11
Bridgewater Clo. PL6—2C 14
Bridwell Clo. PL5—3B 12
Bridwell La. N. PL5—3C 12
Bridwell Rd. PL5—2C 12
Brimhill Clo. PL7—2H 25
Brismar Wlk. PL6—4E 15
Britannia Pl. PL4—3D 22
Brixham Wlk. PL6—3G 15
Brixton Lodge Gdns. PL8
—2F 29
Broadland Gdns. PL9—5A 24
Broadland La. PL9—5H 23
Broadlands Clo. PL7—2G 25
Broad Pk. PL9—6E 23
Broad Pk. Rd. PL3—5H 13
Broad Wlk. PL12—2E 11
Broadway, The. PL9—6G 23
Brockhole La. PL7—3E 17
Brockley Rd. PL3—6E 15
Brockton Gdns. PL6—3D 6
Bromhead Ct. PL6—3C 14
Bromley Pl. PL2—1E 21
Bronte Clo. PL6—2G 13
Brook Clo. PL7—2G 25
Brook Clo. PL12—1G 11
Brookdown Ter. PL12—5E 3
Brookfield Clo. PL7—6H 17
Brooking Clo. PL6—3C 14
Brookingfield Clo. PL7—6C 16
Brooks Hill. PL12—5E 3
Brookwood Rd. PL9—6D 24
Broomfield Dri. PL9—1D 26
Broom Hill. PL12—1D 10
Broom Pk. PL9—2F 27
Broughton Clo. PL3—4B 14
Browning Rd. PL2—6E 13
Brownlow St. PL1—4E 21
(in two parts)
Broxton Dri. PL9—4G 23
Brunel Av. PL2—6D 12
Brunel Rd. PL12—5C 2
Brunel Ter. PL2—6D 12
Brunel Way. PL1—4F 21
Brunswick Pl. PL2—1D 20
Brunswick Rd. PL4—4B 22
(in two parts)
Brynmoor Clo PL3—4C 14
Brynmoor Rd. PL3—4C 14
Brynmoor Wlk. PL3—5C 14
Buckfast Clo. PL2—3D 12

Buckingham Pl. PL5—1B 12
Buckland Clo. PL7—4C 16
Buckland St. PL1—4G 21
Buckwell St. PL1—4A 22
Buddle Clo. PL9—2A 28
Budleigh Clo. PL9—2H 27
Budshead Grn. PL5—5G 5
Budshead Rd. PL5 & PL6—6D 4
Budshead Way. PL5—1A 14
Buena Vista Clo. PL6—2F 7
Buena Vista Dri. PL6—3E 7
Buena Vista Gdns. PL6—3E 7
Buena Vista Way. PL6—3E 7
Bulleid Clo. PL2—4D 12
Buller Clo. PL7—1F 25
Buller Pk. PL12—6D 2
Buller St. PL1—4A 22
Bull Point Cotts. PL5—3H 11
Bulmer Rd. PL4—3C 22
Bulteel Gdns. PL6—2A 6
Bunyan Clo. PL5—1G 13
Burleigh La. PL3—4H 13
Burleigh Pk. Rd. PL3—5H 13
Burnard Clo. PL6—2A 6
Burnet Rd. PL6—3B 14
Burnett Rd. PL12—1D 10
Burnham Pk. Rd. PL3—4H 13
Burniston Clo. PL7—2G 25
Burns Av. PL5—1F 13
Burrington Rd. PL5—2E 13
Burrington Way. PL5—2E 13
Burrow Hill. PL9—1G 27
Burton Clo. PL6—3D 6
Burwell Clo. PL6—5G 7
Bute Rd. PL4—1B 22
Butler Clo. PL6—3C 6
Butterdown. PL12—6B 2
Butt Pk. Rd. PL5—1F 13
Byard Clo. PL5—2C 12
Byland Rd. PL3—5C 14
Byron Av. PL5—1F 13
Bytre Gdns. PL2—4E 13

Cabot Clo. PL12—1E 11
Cadover Clo. PL6—2C 14
Caernarvon Gdns. PL2—4F 13
Calder Clo. PL3—5D 14
Caldicot Gdns. PL6—1D 6
Caledonia Clo. PL7—6H 17
California Gdns. PL3—5F 15
Callington Rd. PL12—5C 2
Calvez Clo. PL10—6F 19
Camarthen Rd. PL4—3C 22
Camber Rd. PL1—5E 21
Camborne Clo. PL5—4E 5
Cambridge Rd. PL2—6D 12
Cambridge Ter. PL11—3H 19
Camden St. PL4—3A 22
Camilla Ter. PL2—4H 13
Campbell Rd. PL9—6H 23
Camperdown St. PL2—1C 20
Campion View. PL6—1G 7
Canefield Av. PL7—2H 25
Canhaye Clo. PL7—2G 25
Cann Gdns. PL6—3H 5
Cannon St. PL1—3B 20
Cann Wood View. PL6—2G 7
Canterbury Clo. PL5—5F 5
Caradon Clo. PL6—5C 6
Carbeile Rd. PL11—2G 19
Cardiff Clo. PL7—1H 25
Cardigan Rd. PL6—2E 15
Cardinal Av. PL5—3B 12
Careswell Av. PL2—3D 12
Carew Av. PL5—6F 5
Carew Gdns. PL5—6F 5
Carew Gdns. PL12—6D 2
Carew Gro. PL5—6F 5
Carew Ter. PL11—3H 19
Carisbroke Rd. PL6—3E 15
Carlisle Rd. PL5—6G 5
Carlton Clo. PL3—6C 14
Carlton Ter. PL4—3B 22
Carlton Ter. PL5—3C 12
Carlyon Clo. PL11—2F 19
Carnock Rd. PL2—3H 13
Carnoustie Dri. PL12—1C 10

Carolina Gdns. PL2—4D 12
Caroline Pl. PL1—4E 21
Carpenter Rd. PL9—5H 23
Carradale Rd. PL6—4E 15
Carroll Rd. PL5—6G 5
Castle Acre Gdns. PL3—6D 14
Castle Bank Gdns. PL3—6D 14
Castle Carey Gdns. PL3—6D 14
Castle Ct. PL12—1C 10
Castlehayes Gdns. PL7—1E 25
Castle La. PL7—1E 25
Castlemead Clo. PL12—6D 2
Castlemead Dri. PL12—6D 2
Castle Rise. PL3—1D 22
Castlerise. PL12—2C 10
Castle St. PL1—4A 22
Castleton Clo. PL3—1C 22
Castleview. PL12—2C 10
Cathcart Av. PL4—3D 22
Catherine St. PL1—4H 21
Cattedown Rd. PL4—4C 22
(in two parts)
Catterick Clo. PL5—4C 4
Cattewater Rd. PL4—4D 22
Cavendish Rd. PL4—4D 22
Caxton Gdns. PL5—2G 13
Cecil Av. PL4—2C 22
Cecil St. PL1—2G 21
Cedar Av. PL9—2E 27
Cedar Clo. PL11—3E 19
Cedar Ct. PL12—1F 11
Cedarcroft Rd. PL2—4F 13
Cedar Dri. PL11—3E 19
Central Pk. Av. PL4—2G 21
Central Rd. PL1—5G 21
Central St. PL1—3F 21
Chaddlewood Av. PL4—2B 22
Chaddlewood Clo. PL7—6F 17
Chagford Wlk. PL6—3G 15
Challgood Clo. PL9—2H 27
Challgood Rise. PL9—2H 27
Challock Clo. PL6—5E 7
Chamberlayne Dri. PL7—5E 17
Channel Pk. Av. PL3—6D 14
Channel View Ter. PL4—2C 22
Chapel Clo. PL12—6B 2
Chapel Row. PL11—2H 19
Chapel St. PL1—3C 20
Chapel Way. PL3—5C 14
Chapeldown Rd. PL11—3G 19
Chapman Ct. PL12—6B 2
Chapmans Ope. PL1—3B 20
Chard Rd. PL5—1B 12
Charfield Dri. PL6—3B 14
Charles Cross. PL4—3A 22
Charles St. PL4—3A 22
Charles Ter. PL3—5C 14
Charlotte St. PL2—1C 20
Charlton Cres. PL6—1C 14
Charlton Rd. PL6—6B 6
Charnhill Clo. PL9—1A 28
Charnhill Way. PL9—1A 28
Chatsworth Gdns. PL5—6D 4
Chaucer Way. PL5—2F 13
Chedworth St. PL4—3A 22
Chelmer Clo. PL7—6G 17
Chelmsford Pl. PL5—5G 5
Chelson Gdns. PL6—6G 7
Cheltenham Pl. PL4—2A 22
Chepstow Av. PL6—1E 7
Cheriton Clo. PL6—6E 5
Cherry Pk. PL7—2G 25
Cherry Tree Dri. PL8—2G 29
Cherrytree La. PL7—1G 25
Chesterfield Rd. PL3—6D 14
Chester Pl. PL4—1A 22
Chesterton Clo. PL5—6G 5
Chestnut Av. PL2—2E 27
Chestnut Clo. PL11—2F 19
Chestnut Rd. PL3—4H 13
Chichester Cres. PL11—1E 11
Childrey Gdns. PL6—2E 15
Childrey Wlk. PL6—2E 15
Chilton Clo. PL6—3D 14
Chittleburn Hill. PL8—1E 29
Chivenor Av. PL5—5B 4
Chubb Dri. PL3—1E 21
Chudleigh Rd. PL4—1C 22

Church Clo. PL7—4B 16
Church Hill. PL6—2C 14
Church Hill Rd. PL6—1C 26
Churchill Wlk. PL12—2E 11
Churchill Way. PL3—5A 14
Churchlands Clo. PL6—2G 7
Churchlands Rd. PL6—1G 7
Church La. PL12—1F 3
Church La. PL11—3A 18
(Antony)
Church La. PL11—5B 18
(St John)
Church Path. PL1—3E 21
Church Pk. Ct. PL6—1G 7
Church Pk. Rd. PL6—1G 7
Church Rd. PL7—1E 25
Church Rd. PL3—6G 23
Church Rd. PL12—2D 10
Church Row La. PL5—3G 5
Churchstow Wlk. PL6—2G 15
Church St. PL3—1E 21
Churchtown Vale. PL12—1D 10
Church Way. PL5—3C 12
Citadel Ope. PL1—4A 22
Citadel Rd. PL1—4G 21
Claremont St. PL1—2G 21
Clarence Ct. PL1—3F 21
Clarence Pl. PL1—3F 21
Clarence Pl. PL2—1C 20
Clarence Pl. PL11—2H 19
Clarence Rd. PL1—2G 19
Clarendon La. PL1—2D 20
Clare Pl. PL4—4B 22
Clayton Pl. PL4—3D 22
Clayton Rd. PL4—3D 22
Clearbrook Av. PL5—2B 12
Clear View. PL12—6E 3
Cleeve Gdns. PL2—3E 13
Clegg Av. PL11—2E 19
Clement Rd. PL7—6H 17
Clevedon Pk. Av. PL2—5F 13
Cleveland Rd. PL4—3C 22
Clieton Pl. PL2—4E 13
Clifford Clo. PL5—1C 12
Cliff Rd. PL1—5G 21
Clifton Av. PL7—4E 17
Clifton Clo. PL7—4E 17
Clifton St. PL4—2A 22
Clinton Av. PL4—2C 22
Clittaford Rd. PL6—3A 6
Close, The. PL12—6C 2
Clovelly Rd. PL4—5C 22
Clovelly View. PL6—6C 22
Clover Rise. PL6—1G 7
Clowance La. PL1—4C 20
Clowance St. PL1—4C 20
Clyde St. PL2—5D 12
Coach Ho. M. PL9—1B 28
Cobbett Rd. PL5—1F 13
Cobb La. PL9—1H 27
Cobourg St. PL1—2H 21
Cockington Clo. PL6—2G 15
Cockington Wlk. PL6—2E 15
Colbourne Rd. PL6—1C 14
Coldrenick St. PL5—2A 12
Colebrook La. PL7—4E 17
Colebrook La. PL7—5B 12
Colebrook Rd. PL7—5E 17
Coleman Dri. PL9—2H 27
Coleridge Av. PL6—1B 14
Coleridge La. PL6—6C 6
Coleridge Rd. PL4—1B 22
Colesdown Hill. PL9—5H 23
Colin Campbell Ct. PL1—3G 21
Collaford Clo. PL7—2G 25
Collard St. PL7—2G 9
College Av. PL4—6A 14
College Dean Clo. PL6—4E 7
College Pk. Pl. PL3—6H 13
College Rd. PL2—6C 12
College View. PL5—6H 13
Collin Clo. PL5—2B 12
Collingwood Av. PL4—4C 22
Collingwood Rd. PL1—2E 21
Colne Gdns. PL3—6D 14
Colston Clo. PL6—3D 6
Coltishall Clo. PL5—5D 4
Coltness Rd. PL9—2B 28

Colwill Rd. PL6—6G 7
Colwill Wlk. PL6—6G 7
Colwin Rd. PL11—2G 19
Combe La. PL7—4E 17
Combley Dri. PL6—5F 7
Commercial Ope. PL4—4B 22
Commercial Rd. PL4—4B 22
Commercial St. PL4—4B 22
Compass Dri. PL7—4G 17
Compton Av. PL3—5D 14
Compton Knoll Clo. PL3—5C 14
Compton Leigh. PL3—5C 14
Compton Pk. Rd. PL3—6B 14
Compton Vale. PL3—6C 14
Congreve Gdns. PL5—2G 13
Coniston Gdns. PL6—5B 6
Connaught Av. PL4—1A 22
Connaught La. PL4—1A 22
Conrad Rd. PL5—2G 13
Constantine St. PL4—3A 22
Convent Clo. PL6—2E 3
Conway Gdns. PL2—3F 13
Conyngham Ct. PL6—3B 14
Cooban Ct. PL6—3C 14
Cook Ct. PL12—6B 2
Cookworthy Rd. PL2—5D 12
Coombe La. PL5 & PL6—3G 5
Coombe Pk. PL12—1F 11
Coombe Pk. La. PL6—6E 5
Coombe Rd. PL12—1F 11
Coombe View. PL2—4C 12
Copice Wood Dri. PL6—1E 7
Coplestone Rd. PL6—4H 5
Coppard Wlk. PL7—6F 17
Copper Beech Way. PL6—2E 7
Coppers Pk. PL6—2G 7
Coppice Gdns. PL5—1H 17
Copse Rd. PL7—1D 24
Copse Rd. PL7—1D 24
Copthorne Gdns. PL9—2H 27
Corea Ter. PL1—3E 21
Corfe Av. PL3—4B 14
Coringdon Clo. PL6—3D 6
Corner Brake. PL6—2F 7
Cornwall Beach. PL1—3B 20
Cornwall St. PL1—3B 20
(Devonport)
Cornwall St. PL1—3G 21
(Plymouth Centre)
Cornwood Rd. PL7—1H 25
Cornworthy Clo. PL2—4E 13
Coronation Pl. PL5—3C 12
Corondale Rd. PL4—4F 13
Corporation Rd. PL2—4H 13
Corsham Clo. PL6—3D 6
Cosdon Pl. PL6—2B 14
Cotehele Av. PL2—6D 12
Cotehele Av. PL4—4D 22
(off Cavendish Rd.)
Cotehele Av. PL4—4C 22
(off Tintern Av.)
Cot Hill. PL7—5B 16
Cot Hill Clo. PL7—5A 16
Cot Hill Dri. PL7—6B 16
Cotton Clo. PL7—1F 25
Coultsfield Clo. PL12—3D 14
County Clo. PL7—6G 17
Courtenay St. PL1—3H 21
Courtfield Rd. PL3—6B 14
Courtland Cres. PL7—4C 16
Courtlands. PL12—2E 11
Court, The. PL6—3E 7
Court, The. PL12—1C 10
Court View. PL8—3F 29
Coverdale Pl. PL7—4A 16
Cowdray Clo. PL12—1E 11
Coypool Rd. PL7—4A 16
Crabtree Clo. PL3—6H 15
Crabtree Vs. PL3—6G 15
Crackston Clo. PL6—4D 14
Craigmore Av. PL2—6D 12
Cramber Clo. PL6—1E 7
Cranbourne Av. PL4—2C 22
Cranfield. PL7—5B 16
Cranmere Rd. PL3—5C 14
Crantock Ter. PL5—1G 13
Craven Av. PL4—2C 22
Crawford Rd. PL1—2F 21

Crediton Wlk. PL6—3G 15
Creedy Rd. PL3—6E 15
Cremyll Rd. PL11—3H 19
Cremyll St. PL1—5E 21
Crescent Av. PL1—4G 21
Crescent, The. PL1—4G 21
Crescent, The. PL8—2C 29
Cressbrook Clo. PL6—1H 15
Cressbrook Dri. PL6—1G 15
Cressbrook Wlk. PL6—1G 15
Cresthill Rd. PL2—4F 13
Croft Rd. PL7—1E 7
Cromer Clo. PL6—2C 6
Cromer Wlk. PL6—2C 6
Cromwell Ga. PL6—2E 7
Cromwell Rd. PL4—4B 22
Crookder Clo. PL2—3A 28
Cross Hill. PL2—1C 20
Cross Pk. PL8—2H 29
Cross Pk. Av. PL6—2A 14
Cross Pk. Rd. PL6—2B 14
Cross Pk. Way. PL6—2B 14
Crossway. PL7—4C 16
Crossway Av. PL4—2D 22
Crowndale Av. PL3—5C 14
Crownhill Fort Rd. PL6—1B 14
Crownhill Rd. PL6—6C 4
Crow Pk. PL3—6B 14
Croydon Gdns. PL5—5C 4
Crozier Rd. PL4—1B 22
Cuffe Rd. PL3—1F 21
Culdrose Clo. PL5—6C 4
Culme Rd. PL3—6C 14
Culver Clo. PL6—3C 14
Culver Rd. PL12—1F 11
Culver Way. PL6—3B 14
Culverwood Clo. PL7—5H 17
Cumberland Rd. PL1—4D 20
Cumberland St. PL1—3C 20
Cundy Clo. PL7—4A 16
Cunningham Rd. PL5—1G 5
Curtis St. PL1—4C 20
Cypress Clo. PL7—6H 17

Dale Av. PL6—4E 15
Dale Gdns. PL6—1H 21
Dale Rd. PL4—1H 21
Dalton Gdns. PL5—6C 4
Danum Dri. PL7—2H 25
Dark St. La. PL7—6E 17
Dart Clo. PL3—4F 15
Dartington Wlk. PL6—3G 15
Dartmeet Av. PL3—5D 14
Dartmoor View. PL4—2E 23
Dartmouth Wlk. PL6—3F 15
Darwin Cres. PL3—5D 14
Davenham Clo. PL6—3D 6
David Clo. PL7—5F 17
Davy Clo. PL11—2F 19
Dawes La. PL9—6C 23
Dawlish Wlk. PL6—3G 15
Dawson Clo. PL5—2C 12
Daymond Rd. PL5—1B 12
Dayton Clo. PL6—6A 6
Deacon Clo. PL12—2F 11
Deacon Dri. PL12—2F 11
Dean Cross. PL9—6G 23
Dean Cross Rd. PL9—6G 23
Dean Hill. PL9—6G 23
Dean Pk. Rd. PL9—6F 23
Dean Rd. PL7—4D 16
Debble Clo. PL7—4E 17
Debden Clo. PL5—5B 4
Deep La. PL7—2H 25
Deer Pk. PL12—6F 3
Deer Pk. Dri. PL3—5E 15
Defoe Clo. PL5—2G 13
Delacombe Rd. PL7—4F 17
Delamere Rd. PL6—4E 15
Delaware Gdns. PL2—4D 12
Dell, The. PL7—5B 16
Dengie Clo. PL7—6H 17
Denham Clo. PL5—1G 13
Dennis Clo. PL5—4A 12
Deptford Pl. PL4—2A 22

Derby Rd. PL5—5G 5
Derriford Pk. PL6—6C 6
Derriford Rd. PL6—5C 6
Derry Av. PL4—2H 21
Derry's Cross. PL1—4G 21
Derwent Av. PL3—6D 14
Desborough Rd. PL4—3B 22
Deveron Clo. PL7—6G 17
Devonia Rd. PL7—4E 17
Devonport Hill. PL1—4D 20
Devonport Rd. PL1 & PL3
—3D 20
Devonshire St. PL4—3A 22
Devon Ter. PL3—6H 13
Dewar Wlk. PL5—1D 12
Diamond Av. PL4—2B 22
Dickens Rd. PL5—1F 13
Dickiemoor La. PL5—1F 13
Dieppe Clo. PL1—3C 20
Digby Gro. PL5—4C 4
Dingle Rd. PL2—5E 13
Dingle Rd. PL7—5C 16
Dingwall Av. PL5—6A 6
Dirty La. PL12—4B 2
Distine Rd. PL3—4D 14
Dittisham Wlk. PL6—3G 15
Ditton Ct. PL6—3C 14
Dixon Pl. PL2—1D 20
Dockray Clo. PL6—5F 7
Doddridge Clo. PL3—4F 15
Dolphin Clo. PL9—6H 23
Dolphin Ct. Rd. PL9—1H 27
Dolphin Sq. PL9—6H 23
Donnington Dri. PL3—4D 14
Dorchester Av. PL5—5H 5
Doreena Rd. PL9—6C 24
Dormy Av. PL3—6B 14
Dorsmouth Ter. PL7—1E 25
Douglas Dri. PL9—1A 28
Douglass Rd. PL3—5E 15
Dovedale Rd. PL2—4E 13
Dove Gdns. PL3—4F 15
Dover Rd. PL6—6G 7
Down Clo. PL12—2C 10
Downfield Dri. PL7—6F 17
Downfield Wlk. PL7—6F 17
Downgate Gdns. PL2—3H 13
Downham Gdns. PL5—2G 5
Downhorn Pk. PL9—6G 23
Down Rd. PL7—6G 17
Downside Av. PL6—4D 14
Drake Circus. PL4—3H 21
Drakefield Dri. PL12—6F 3
Drake's Clo. PL6—4B 6
Drake Way. PL9—6G 23
Drax Gdns. PL6—3A 14
Drayton Rd. PL5—2G 13
Drew Clo. PL12—1B 10
Drive, The. PL3—4A 14
Drummond Clo. PL2—4D 12
Drummond Pl. PL1—2D 20
Drunken Bri. Hill. PL7—2C 24
Dryburgh Cres. PL2—3E 13
Dryden Av. PL5—2G 13
Duckworth St. PL2—1E 21
Dudley Gdns. PL6—3D 14
Dudley Rd. PL7—6B 16
Duke St. PL1—3C 20
Duloe Gdns. PL2—3G 13
Dumfries Av. PL5—6H 5
Duncan St. PL1—4C 20
Dunclair Pk. PL3—6F 15
Duncombe Av. PL5—6D 4
Dundas St. PL2—1E 21
Dundonald St. PL2—1D 20
Dunheved Rd. PL12—1E 11
Dunkes Well Clo. PL2—3D 12
Dunley Wlk. PL6—2E 15
Dunnet Rd. PL6—3H 5
Dunnock Way. PL12—6C 2
Dunraven Dri. PL6—4B 6
Dunster Clo. PL7—1H 25
Dunstone Av. PL9—6A 24
Dunstone Clo. PL9—6H 23
Dunstone Clo. PL9—6H 23
Dunstone La. PL9—6B 24
Dunstone Rd. PL5—6D 4
Dunstone Rd. PL9—6H 23

Dunstone View. PL9—6A 24
Durban Rd. PL3—6H 13
Durham Av. PL4—2C 22
Durnford St. PL1—4E 21
Durnford St. Ope. PL1—4E 21
Durrant Clo. PL1—2C 20
Durris Clo. PL6—5F 7
Durris Gdns. PL6—5F 7
Duxford Clo. PL5—4C 4
Dynevor Clo. PL3—4B 14

Earl's Acre. PL3—1F 21
Earls Mill Rd. PL7—5E 17
Earls Wood Clo. PL6—6H 7
Earls Wood Dri. PL6—6H 7
Eastbury Gro. PL6—1E 13
Eastcote Clo. PL6—3D 6
Easterdown Clo. PL9—6H 23
Eastfield Av. PL9—1E 27
Eastfield Cres. PL3—4C 14
Eastlake St. PL1—3H 21
Eastlake Wlk. PL1—3A 22
East, Pk. Av. PL4—1H 21
East St. PL1—4F 21
Ebrington St. PL4—3A 22
Eddystone Ter. PL1—5G 21
Edgar Ter. PL4—1C 22
Edgcumbe Ct. PL1—2E 21
Edgcumbe Cres. PL10—6F 19
Edgcumbe Pk. Rd. PL3—5H 13
Edgcumbe St. PL1—4E 21
Edinburgh St. PL1—3C 20
Edith Av. PL4—2C 22
Edith St. PL5—2B 12
Edwards Clo. PL7—1H 25
Edwards Cres. PL12—1B 10
Edwards Dri. PL7—6H 17
Effingham Cres. PL3—4H 13
Efford Cres. PL3—5D 14
Efford La. PL3—1D 22
Efford Pathway. PL3—5E 15
Efford Rd. PL3—5D 14
Efford Wlk. PL7—6F 17
Egerton Cres. PL4—3C 22
Egerton Pl. PL4—3C 22
Egerton Rd. PL4—3B 22
Eggbuckland Rd. PL6 & PL3
—3D 14
Eight Acres Clo. PL7—6H 17
Elaine Clo. PL7—1B 24
Elburton Rd. PL9—5A 24
Eldad Hill. PL1—3F 21
Elder Clo. PL7—6H 17
Elford Cres. PL7—4E 17
Elford Dri. PL9—6E 23
Elgin Cres. PL5—6A 6
Elim Ter. PL3—6A 14
Eliot St. PL5—3C 12
Elizabeth Pl. PL4—2A 22
Elliot Clo. PL12—1D 10
Elliot Rd. PL4—4C 22
Elliot Sq. PL11—2H 19
Elliot St. PL1—4G 21
Elliot Ter. PL1—5G 21
Elliot Ter. La. PL1—5G 21
Elm Cres. PL3—1C 22
Elmcroft. PL2—4F 13
Elm Gro. PL6—6E 17
Elm Rd. PL4—6B 14
Elm Rd. PL6—3F 7
Elms, The. PL3—2E 21
Elms, The. PL12—1A 2
Elmwood Clo. PL6—4F 7
Elphinstone Rd. PL2—4G 13
Elton Ter. PL1—3G 21
Elwell Rd. PL12—6G 3
Elwick Gdns. PL3—6D 14
Embankment La. PL4—3D 22
Embankment Rd. PL4—4C 22
Emma Pl. PL1—4E 21
Emma Pl. Ope. PL1—4E 21
Endsleigh Pl. PL4—2H 21
Endsleigh Pk. Rd. PL3—5H 13
Endsleigh Rd. PL9—6E 23
Ennerdale Gdns. PL6—5A 6

Epping Cres. PL6—4F 15
Epworth Ter. PL2—6D 12
Eric Rd. PL4—3C 22
Erith Av. PL2—6F 13
Erle Gdns. PL7—2F 25
Erlstoke Clo. PL6—2F 15
Erme Gdns. PL3—6E 15
Ermington Ter. PL4—1A 22
Ernesettle Cres. PL5—6B 4
Ernesettle Grn. PL5—4C 4
Ernesettle La. PL5—4B 4
Ernesettle Rd. PL5—6C 4
Esmonde Gdns. PL5—3H 11
Esplanade, The. PL1—5H 21
Essa Rd. PL12—1F 11
Essex St. PL1—2G 21
Esso Wharf Rd. PL4—5C 22
Estover Clo. PL6—5H 7
Estover Rd. PL6—5H 7
Eton Av. PL1—2H 21
Eton Pl. PL1—2H 21
Eton St. PL1—2H 21
Evans Pl. PL2—6F 13
Evelyn Pl. PL4—2A 22
Evelyn St. PL5—2B 12
Exchange St. PL4—4A 22
Exe Gdns. PL3—4E 15
Exeter Clo. PL5—5B 4
Exeter St. PL4—3A 22
Exmouth Rd. PL1—2D 20
(in two parts)

Fairfax Ter. PL2—1D 20
Fairfield. PL7—4D 16
Fairfield Av. PL2—4G 13
Fairmead Clo. PL12—1A 2
Fairmead Rd. PL12—1C 10
Fairmede M. PL12—1C 10
Fairview Av. PL3—6F 15
Fairview Way. PL3—6G 15
Fairway. PL12—1C 10
Fanshawe Way. PL9—1E 27
Faraday Rd. PL4—4D 22
Farm Clo. PL4—4C 16
Farm La. PL5—1F 13
Farnley Clo. PL6—3D 6
Farringdon Rd. PL4—2C 22
Federation Rd. PL3—6E 15
Fegen Rd. PL5—2H 11
Fellowes Pl. PL1—3E 21
Fenten Pk. PL12—6F 3
Ferndale Av. PL2—4C 12
Ferndale Clo. PL6—1F 7
Ferndale Rd. PL2—4C 12
Fernleigh Rd. PL3—6B 14
Fernside Way. PL12—6C 2
Ferrers Rd. PL5—2C 12
Ferry La. PL11—5D 10
Ferry Rd. PL1—2B 20
Ferry St. PL11—2A 20
Feversham Clo. PL7—5G 17
Finch Clo. PL3—1E 23
Finches Clo. PL9—6C 24
Findon Gdns. PL6—5F 7
Fineswell St. PL1—4H 21
Fircroft Rd. PL2—4H 13
First Av. PL1—3E 21
First Av. PL9—5H 23
Fisher Rd. PL2—6E 13
Fistral Clo. PL11—1F 19
Fitzroy Rd. PL1—2E 21
Fitzroy Ter. PL1—2E 21
Flamborough Rd. PL6—2C 6
Flamborough Way. PL6—2C 6
Flamsteed Cres. PL5—2C 12
Fleet St. PL2—5C 12
Fletcher Cres. PL9—1A 28
Fletcher Way. PL9—1A 28
Fletemoor Rd. PL5—2B 12
Flora Cotts. PL1—4G 21
Flora St. PL1—4G 21
Florence Pl. PL4—3C 22
Florence St. PL5—2D 12
Foliot Av. PL2—5E 13
Foliot Rd. PL2—4D 12
Forder Heights. PL6—2D 14
Forder Valley Rd. PL6—2D 14

Ford Hill. PL2—6E 13
Ford Pk. PL4—1A 22
Ford Pk. La. PL4—6A 14
Ford Pk. Rd. PL4—1H 21
Forest Av. PL2—4G 13
Foresters Dri. PL6—2F 7
Foresters Rd. PL9—6F 23
Fore St. PL1—3C 20
Fore St. PL5—3F 5
Fore St. PL7—1E 25
Fore St. PL11—2A 20
Fore St. PL12—1F 11
Forest View. PL6—2F 7
Fort Austin Av. PL6—1B 14
Fortescue Pl. PL3—5C 14
Forth Gdns. PL3—4F 15
Fort Ter. PL6—6B 6
Fosbrooke Ct. PL3—5B 14
Foulston Av. PL5—2A 12
Fountains Cres. PL2—3F 13
Fowey Gdns. PL3—4F 15
Foxfield Clo. PL3—6E 15
Foxtor Clo. PL5—6F 5
Foxwood Gdns. PL6—4A 6
Foxwood Gdns. PL9—2G 27
Foyle Clo. PL7—6G 17
Francis St. PL1—3F 21
Frankfort Ga. PL1—3G 21
Franklyns. PL6—5C 6
Franklyns Clo. PL6—5C 6
Fraser Pl. PL5—2F 5
Fraser Rd. PL5—2G 5
Fraser Sq. PL5—2F 5
Frederick St. E. PL1—3G 21
Frederick St. W. PL1—3F 21
Fredington Grn. PL2—5F 13
Fremantle Pl. PL2—1D 20
Frensham Av. PL6—2E 7
Frensham Gdns. PL6—2E 7
Freshford Clo. PL6—2E 15
Freshford Wlk. PL6—2E 15
Frewin Gdns. PL6—3C 6
Friars La. PL1—4A 22
Frith Rd. PL2—6D 2
Frobisher Dri. PL12—1E 11
Frogmore Av. PL6—3D 14
Frogmore Rd. PL6—4D 14
Frome Clo. PL7—1G 25
Frontfield Cres. PL6—4A 6
Fullerton Rd. PL2—6E 13
Furland Clo. PL9—2E 27
Furneaux Av. PL2—6F 13
Furneaux Rd. PL2—5F 13
Fursdon Clo. PL9—1C 28
Furse Pk. PL5—4A 12
Furzeacre Clo. PL7—4G 17
Furzehatt Av. PL9—1A 28
Furzehatt Pk. Rd. PL9—1A 28
Furzehatt Rise. PL9—1A 28
Furzehatt Rd. PL9—1H 27
Furzehatt Vs. PL9—1H 27
Furzehatt Way. PL9—1A 28
Furzehill Rd. PL4—1B 22

Gabber La. PL9—6E 27
Galileo Clo. PL7—5E 17
Gallacher Way. PL12—6B 2
Galsworthy Clo. PL5—1G 13
Ganges Rd. PL2—6E 13
Ganna Pk. Rd. PL3—5H 13
Gara Clo. PL9—1B 28
Garden Cres. PL1—5G 21
Garden Pk. Clo. PL9—6B 24
Garden St. PL2—1C 20
Garden Village. PL9—5H 23
Gards La. PL5—1C 12
Garfield Ter. PL2—1D 20
Garrick Clo. PL5—1G 13
Garston Clo. PL9—5A 24
Gascoyne Pl. PL4—3A 22
Gashouse La. PL4—4B 22
Gasking St. PL4—3A 22
Gdynia Way. PL4—4B 22
Geasons La. PL7—6E 17
George Av. PL7—5E 17
George La. PL7—1F 25
George Pl. PL1—4F 21

George St. PL1—4D 20
Gibbon La. PL4—3A 22
Gibbon St. PL4—3A 22
Gifford Pl. PL3—1H 21
Gifford Ter. Rd. PL3—6H 13
Gilbert Ct. PL7—6H 17
Gilbert La. PL2—6F 13
Gill Pk. PL3—6D 14
Gilston Rd. PL12—5C 2
Gilwell Av. PL9—6A 24
Gilwell St. PL4—3A 22
Glanville St. PL4—3H 21
Glanville Ter. PL12—6F 3
Glebe Av. PL12—6F 3
Glenavon Rd. PL3—6A 14
Glenburn Clo. PL3—4A 14
Glendower Rd. PL3—6H 13
Gleneagle Av. PL3—5B 14
Gleneagle Rd. PL3—5B 14
Glenfield Rd. PL6—4E 7
Glenfield Way. PL6—4F 7
Glenhaven Clo. PL7—5H 17
Glenholt Clo. PL6—3F 7
Glenholt Rd. PL6—3E 7
Glenhurst Rd. PL3—5A 14
Glenmore Av. PL2—6D 12
Glen Pk. Av. PL4—2H 21
Glen Rd. PL3—6B 14
Glen Rd. PL7—5D 16
Glentor Rd. PL3—4H 13
Glenwood Rd. PL3—5A 14
Gloucester Ct. PL1—2H 21
Gloucester Pl. PL1—2H 21
Goad Av. PL4—4C 22
Goad Av. PL11—2E 19
Goad Clo. PL11—2F 19
Godding Gdns. PL6—3A 6
Golden Sq. PL7—5E 17
Goodeve Clo. PL9—1G 27
Goodwin Av. PL6—3C 6
Goodwin Cres. PL2—5E 13
Gooseberry La. PL1—4G 21
Gooseford La. PL11—4C 18
Goosewell Hill. PL6—3D 14
Goosewell Pk. Rd. PL9—1H 27
Goosewell Rd. PL9—1H 27
Goosewell Ter. PL9—1H 27
Gordon La. PL4—1H 21
Gordon Ter. PL4—1H 21
Gorsey Clo. PL5—1A 14
Goswela Clo. PL9—2H 27
Goswela Gdns. PL9—2H 27
Gower Ridge Rd. PL9—1F 27
Grafton Rd. PL4—1A 22
Grainge Rd. PL6—2B 14
Granby Ct. PL1—3C 20
Granby Grn. PL1—3C 20
Granby Pl. PL1—3C 20
Granby St. PL1—3C 20
Granby Way. PL1—3C 20
Grand Hotel Rd. PL1—5G 21
Grand Pde. PL1—5G 21
Grange Rd. PL7—1F 25
Grantham Clo. PL7—1B 24
Grantley Gdns. PL3—6C 14
Grasmere Clo. PL6—4A 6
Grassendale Av. PL2—4D 12
Gratton Clo. PL2—2C 14
Gravesend Gdns. PL11—2H 19
Gravesend Wlk. PL5—5B 4
Gray Cres. PL5—3A 12
Gt. Berry Rd. PL6—2A 14
Gt. Churchway. PL9—6A 24
Greatfield Rd. PL3—4D 14
Greatlands Cres. PL2—5E 13
Greatlands Pl. PL2—5E 13
Gt. Park Clo. PL7—6H 17
Gt. Western Rd. PL1—5G 21
Grebe Clo. PL7—6F 17
Greenacres. PL9—5H 23
Greenbank Av. PL4—2B 22
Greenbank Rd. PL4—1A 22
Greenbank Ter. PL4—2B 22
Greendale Rd. PL2—4A 14
Greenfield Rd. PL12—1D 10
Greenhill Clo. PL9—2H 27
Greenlees Dri. PL7—2H 25
Green Pk. Av. PL4—1H 21

Green Pk. Rd. PL9—1F 27
Green, The. PL9—1D 26
Green, The. PL12—6C 2
Greenway Av. PL7—4B 16
Greenwood Pk. Clo. PL7—5H 17
Greenwood Pk. Rd. PL7—5H 17
Grenfell Av. PL12—6C 2
Grenfell Gdns. PL12—6C 2
Grenville Clo. PL7—6H 17
Grenville Rd. PL4—3C 22
Gresham Clo. PL5—2G 5
Greystoke Av. PL6—4E 15
Griffin Way. PL9—1B 28
Griggs Clo. PL7—2H 25
Grimspound Clo. PL6—3G 15
Grizedale Rd. PL6—4F 15
Grosvenor Rd. PL6—1B 14
Grove Pk. PL11—2E 19
Grove, The. PL3—1E 21
Grove, The. PL9—5F 23
Guildford Clo. PL5—6A 6
Guildford St. PL4—1A 22
Gurnard Wlk. PL3—5E 15
Gurney Clo. PL11—2F 19
Gwithian Clo. PL11—1F 19
Gwyn Rd. PL4—2C 22

Haddington Rd. PL2—1C 20
Halcyon Ct. PL2—5E 13
Halcyon Rd. PL2—5E 13
Haldon Pl. PL5—6E 5
Hallerton Clo. PL6—2G 15
Hallet Clo. PL12—6B 2
Halley Gdns. PL3—2C 12
Hamble Clo. PL3—4F 15
Ham Clo. PL2—4G 13
Ham Dri. PL2—4E 13
Ham Grn. Ct. PL2—4E 13
Ham Grn. La. PL2—4E 13
Ham Grn. PL2—4E 13
Hamilton Gdns. PL4—1H 21
Ham La. PL2—4H 13
(in two parts)
Hammick Wlk. PL7—5F 17
Hamoaze Av. PL5—3B 12
Hamoaze Ct. PL1—4C 20
Hamoaze Pl. PL1—3B 20
Hamoaze Rd. PL11—3H 19
Hampton St. PL4—3A 22
Hancock Clo. PL6—3H 5
Hanover Clo. PL3—6D 14
Hanover Rd. PL3—6D 14
Harbour Av. PL4—4A 22
Harbour Av. PL5—4E 15
Harbour St. PL11—2H 19
Harbour View. PL9—6C 22
Harbour View. PL12—1E 11
Hardy Cres. PL5—2A 14
Harewood Clo. PL7—6D 16
Harewood Cres. PL5—1E 13
Hargood Ter. PL2—1D 20
Harlech Clo. PL3—4B 14
Harnolen Rd. PL2—4H 13
Haroldsleigh Av. PL5—1A 14
Harrison St. PL2—1C 20
Hartland Clo. PL6—2C 6
Hartley Av. PL3—5B 14
Hartley Pk. Gdns. PL3—5B 14
Hartley Rd. PL3—5A 14
Hartwell Av. PL9—6D 24
Harvey Pl. PL4—4D 22
Harvey St. PL11—2H 19
Harwell Ct. PL1—3G 21
Harwell St. PL1—3G 21
Harwood Av. PL5—2G 5
Hastings St. PL1—3G 21
Hastings Ter. PL1—3G 21
Haswell Clo. PL6—3C 14
Hatshill Clo. PL6—6H 7
Havelock Ter. PL1—2D 20
Haweswater Clo. PL6—5A 6
Hawkers Av. PL4—3A 22
Hawkers La. PL3—6A 14
Hawkinge Gdns. PL5—5C 4
Hawkins Clo. PL6—4C 6
Hawks Pl. PL12—1C 10
Hawthorn Av. PL11—2F 19

Hawthorn Clo. PL6—2F 7
Hawthorn Clo. PL9—2E 27
Hawthorne Gro. PL2—4G 13
Hawthorns. PL12—1D 10
Haydon Gro. PL5—2A 12
Haye Rd. PL9—3B 24
Haye Rd. S. PL9—6C 24
Hayes Pl. PL6—3D 14
Hayes Rd. PL9—6E 23
Haystone Pl. PL1—2G 21
Haytor Clo. PL5—6F 5
Hazel Clo. PL6—3D 6
Hazel Gro. PL9—5C 24
Hazelwood Cres. PL9—6D 24
Hazelwood Dri. PL6—1F 7
Headland Pk. PL4—2A 22
Healy Pl. PL2—1C 20
Heanl Rd. PL12—6B 2
Heathers, The. PL6—2F 7
Heathfield Rd. PL4—2D 22
Hedgerow Clo. PL6—1G 7
Hedingham Clo. PL7—1H 25
Hedingham Gdns. PL6—2D 6
Hele Gdns. PL7—1F 25
Hele La. PL6—1H 7
Heles Ter. PL4—3D 22
Hemerdon Heights. PL7—5G 17
Hemerdon La. PL7—3H 17
Hemerdon Way. PL7—5D 16
Henderson Pl. PL2—5D 12
Hendwell Clo. PL6—3A 6
Henley Dri. PL5—2G 5
Herbert Pl. PL2—1C 20
Herbert St. PL2—1C 20
Hereford Rd. PL5—4F 5
Heritage Clo. PL12—6C 2
Hermitage Rd. PL3—6A 14
Herschel Gdns. PL5—2C 12
Hertland Wlk. PL2—4E 13
Hessary Dri. PL6—1E 7
Hessary View. PL12—5E 3
Hetling Clo. PL1—3G 21
Hewitt Clo. PL2—2C 10
Hexham Pl. PL2—3D 12
Hexton Hill. PL9—1D 26
Heybrook Av. PL5—2B 12
Hickory Dri. PL7—6H 17
Hicks La. PL4—4A 22
Highbury Cres. PL7—4C 16
Highclere Gdns. PL6—1D 6
Highcombe La. PL9—3E 27
Higher Churchway. PL9—6A 24
Higher Compton Rd. PL3—5B 14
Higher Efford Rd. PL3—6D 14
Higher La. PL1—4H 21
Higher Mowles. PL3—5D 14
Higher Port View. PL12—1E 11
Higher Pk. Clo. PL7—2H 25
Higher Stert Ter. PL4—3C 22
Higher Woodford La. PL7
—4C 16
Highfield Clo. PL3—6E 15
High St. Stonehouse, PL1
—4E 21
Hill Clo. PL7—1D 24
Hill Crest. PL3—6A 14
Hillcrest Clo. PL7—6G 17
Hillcrest Dri. PL7—1G 25
Hilldale Rd. PL6—1G 27
Hilldean Clo. PL5—2G 5
Hill La. PL3—4B 14
Hill Path. PL5—4D 4
Hill Pk. Cres. PL4—2A 22
Hillsborough. PL4—6B 14
Hillsdunne Rd. PL3—5A 14
Hillside Av. PL4—1H 21
Hillside Av. PL12—6F 3
Hillside Cres. PL9—5H 23
Hillside Rd. PL12—6E 3
Hill St. PL4—3A 22
Hilltop Cres. PL5—1C 12
Hilton Av. PL5—2G 13
Hingstone Ct. PL6—3C 14
Hirmandale Rd. PL5—6D 4
Hobart St. PL1—4F 21
Hobbs Cres. PL12—6C 2
Hodge Clo. PL12—1C 10

Hoe Gdns. PL1—4H 21
Hoegate Pl. PL1—4H 21
Hoegate St. PL1—4H 21
Hoe Rd. PL1—5G 21
Hoe St. PL1—4H 21
Hogarth Clo. PL9—1B 28
Hogarth Wlk. PL9—1B 28
Holborn St. PL4—4B 22
Holcombe Dri. PL9—2H 27
Holcroft Clo. PL12—1D 10
Holdsworth St. PL3—2H 21
Holebay Clo. PL9—2A 28
Holland Rd. PL3—5A 14
Holland Rd. PL7—6H 17
Holland Rd. PL9—6H 23
Hollong Pk. PL11—3A 18
Holloway Gdns. PL9—2A 28
Hollowgutter La. PL11—3B 18
Holly Ct. PL6—4G 15
Hollycroft Rd. PL3—4C 14
Holly Pk. Clo. PL5—4E 5
Holly Pk. Dri. PL5—4E 5
Hollywood Ter. PL1—3G 21
Holman Ct. PL2—3G 13
Holmans Bldgs. PL1—3B 20
Holmbush Way. PL8—3G 29
Holmer Down. PL6—2F 7
Holmes Av. PL3—6D 14
Holmwood Av. PL9—2G 27
Holtwood Rd. PL6—3F 7
Holwell Clo. PL9—6H 23
Holyrood Pl. PL1—5H 21
Home Farm Rd. PL9—5G 23
Home Pk. PL2—1D 20
Home Pk. Av. PL3—5A 14
Home Pk. Rd. PL12—6F 3
Homer Pk. PL9—2E 27
Homer Pk. PL12—6D 2
Homer Pk. La. S. PL9—2E 27
Homer Rise. PL9—6B 24
Home Sweet Home Ter. PL4
—4C 22
Honeysuckle Clo. PL6—2G 7
Honicknowle Grn. PL5—4F 5
Honicknowle La. PL2 & PL5
—3G 13
Honiton Clo. PL5—6E 5
Honiton Wlk. PL5—5F 5
Hood St. PL1—2C 20
Hooe Hill. PL9—2D 26
Hooe La. PL9—3E 27
Hooe Rd. PL9—1D 26
Hooksbury Av. PL7—2H 25
Hopton Clo. PL6—3B 14
Hornbeam Clo. PL12—6B 2
Hornbrook Gdns. PL6—3H 5
Hornby St. PL2—1D 20
Hornchurch La. PL5—5C 4
Hornchurch Rd. PL5—4C 4
Horncray Vs. PL9—5F 23
Horn Cross Rd. PL9—6G 23
Horn La. PL9—6G 23
Horn La. Flats. PL9—6H 23
Horsham La. PL5—1G 13
(Honicknowle)
Horsham La. PL5—1F 5
(Tamerton Foliot)
Horswell Clo. PL7—6H 17
Hosford Clo. PL9—3H 27
Hospital Rd. PL4—2A 22
Hotham Pl. PL1—2F 21
Houldsworth Rd. PL9—6E 23
Houndiscombe Rd. PL4—2A 22
Howard Clo. PL12—6D 2
Howard Rd. PL9—6F 23
How St. PL4—4A 22
Hubbard Wlk. PL7—6G 17
Humber Clo. PL5—5F 15
Hungerford Rd. PL2—5E 13
Hunter Clo. PL6—1B 14
Huntington Gdns. PL5—5H 5
Huntley Pl. PL3—1E 23
Huntley Vs. PL3—1E 23
Hurrabrook Clo. PL6—1G 15
Hurrabrook Gdns. PL6—1G 15
Hurrell Clo. PL3—6E 15
Hurrell Clo. PL6—3H 5
Hurril Wlk. PL7—6G 17

Hurst Clo. PL9—2H 27
Hutchings Clo. PL6—3H 5
Huxham Clo. PL6—3C 14
Huxley Clo. PL7—4F 17
Hyde Pk. Rd. PL3—6A 14

Ilbert St. PL1—2G 21
Ince Clo. PL11—1F 19
Inchkeith Rd. PL6—2B 6
Ingra Rd. PL3—5C 14
Ingra Wlk. PL6—1D 6
Instow Wlk. PL5—6E 5
Insworke Cres. PL10—6F 19
Inverdene. PL3—6H 13
Ipswich Clo. PL5—5G 5
Ivanhoe Rd. PL5—1B 12
Ivydale Rd. PL4—1B 22

Jackson Clo. PL5—3D 12
Jackson Pl. PL2—1D 20
Jago Av. PL1—2H 19
James Pl. PL4—2H 21
James St. PL4—2H 21
James St. PL1—4C 20
James St. PL4—2H 21
Jean Cres. PL3—5D 14
Jedburgh Cres. PL2—3E 13
Jeffery Clo. PL6—3H 5
Jenkins Clo. PL9—2A 28
Jenney's Cres. PL12—6B 2
Jennycliff La. PL9—2C 26
Jennyscombe Clo. PL9—3H 27
Jephson Rd. PL4—2D 22
Jessops. PL7—4D 16
Jinkin Av. PL4—2B 22
John La. PL4—2H 21
John St. PL1—2C 20
Jubilee Rd. PL5—6D 4
Julian St. PL4—4C 22
Jump Clo. PL6—1E 7

Kathleaven St. PL5—2B 12
Kay Clo. PL7—4F 17
Keat St. PL2—1C 20
Kedlestone Av. PL5—6E 5
Keen Clo. PL12—1B 10
Keep, The. PL12—1C 10
Kelly Clo. PL5—4A 12
Kelvin Av. PL4—2C 22
Kendal Pl. PL5—5A 6
Kenilworth Rd. PL2—4E 13
Kenley Gdns. PL5—5D 4
Kenmare Dri. PL6—6F 17
Kenn Clo. PL5—6F 5
Kennel Hill. PL7—1D 24
Kennel Hill Clo. PL7—1C 24
Kennet Clo. PL3—5D 14
Kensington Pl. PL4—1B 22
Kensington Rd. PL4—1B 22
Kent Rd. PL2—1D 20
Keppel Pl. PL2—1D 20
Keppel St. PL2—1D 20
Kernow Clo. PL11—2E 19
Ker St. PL1—4C 20
Ker St. Ope. PL1—3C 20
Kestrel Way. PL6—1F 7
Keswick Cres. PL6—1F 15
Keyes Clo. PL1—3C 20
Keyham Rd. PL6—2E 15
Keyham St. PL5—3C 12
Khyber Clo. PL11—2G 19
Kidwelly Clo. PL7—1H 25
Kiel Pl. PL3—6F 15
Killigrew Ave. PL12—2D 10
Kilnpark Wlk. PL11—5D 10
King Edward Rd. PL12—1F 11
Kingsland Gdns. Clo. PL3
—5A 14
Kingsley Av. PL11—3H 19
Kingsley Rd. PL4—1A 22
Kings Rd. PL1—3D 20
Kings Rd. PL5—6D 4
King's Tamerton Rd. PL5
—1C 12

Kingston Clo. PL7—6G 17
Kingston Dri. PL7—6G 17
King St. PL1—3F 21
Kingsway Gdns. PL6—6B 6
Kingswear Cres. PL6—2D 14
Kingswood Pk. Rd. PL3—5H 13
Kinnaird Cres. PL6—2A 6
Kinross Av. PL4—1C 22
Kinsale Rd. PL5—6C 4
Kinterbury Rd. PL5—3H 11
Kinterbury St. PL1—4A 22
Kinterbury Ter. PL5—3H 11
Kinver Clo. PL6—5F 7
Kipling Gdns. PL5—1H 13
Kirkby Pl. PL4—2H 21
Kirkby Ter. PL4—2H 21
Kirkdale Gdns. PL2—4F 13
Kirkland Clo. PL6—2E 7
Kirkstall Clo. PL2—4D 12
Kirkwall Rd. PL5—6A 6
Kirton Pl. PL3—6D 14
Kit Hill. PL5—3A 12
Kit Hill Cres. PL5—3A 12
Kitley Way. PL5—2B 12
Kitter Dri. PL9—2H 27
Knapps Clo. PL9—1C 28
Kneele Gdns. PL3—3A 14
Knighton Rd. PL4—3B 22
Knighton Rd. PL6—6B 28
Knoll, The. PL7—5B 16
Knowland Clo. PL1—2C 20
Knowle Av. PL2—5C 12
Knowle Wlk. PL2—5C 12
Kynance La. PL11—1F 19

Ladysmith Ct. PL4—2C 22
Ladysmith Rd. PL4—2C 22
Laira Av. PL3—1F 23
Laira Bri. Rd. PL4—3D 22
Laira Gdns. PL3—1E 23
Laira Pl. PL4—3C 22
Laira Pk. Cres. PL4—1D 22
Laira Pk. Pl. PL4—1D 22
Laira Pk. Rd. PL4—1D 22
Laira St. PL4—3C 22
Laity Wlk. PL6—3H 5
Lake Rd. PL9—1D 06
Lakeside Dri. PL5—4B 4
Lake View Clo. PL5—4E 5
Lake View Dri. PL5—4E 5
Lalebrick Rd. PL9—2C 26
Lambert Rd. PL5—3F 5
Lambhay Hill. PL1—5A 22
Lambhay St. PL1—5A 22
Lamerton Clo. PL6—6E 5
Lamorna Pk. PL11—2E 19
Lancaster Gdns. PL5—5G 5
Lander Rd. PL12—6F 3
Landrake Clo. PL5—3A 12
Lands Pk. PL9—6H 23
Landulph Gdns. PL5—3A 12
Langdale Clo. PL6—1F 15
Langdale Gdns. PL6—1F 15
Langdon Ct. PL9—1B 28
Langerwell Clo. PL12—6C 2
Langerwell La. PL12—6B 2
Lang Gro. PL9—6B 24
Langham Pl. PL4—3C 22
Langhill Rd. PL3—6H 13
Langley Clo. PL6—2C 6
Langley Cres. PL6—2B 6
Langmead Clo. PL6—3E 15
Langmead Rd. PL6—3E 15
Langmore Clo. PL6—3C 14
Lagoon Down Way. PL11
—2E 19
Langstone Rd. PL2—4G 13
Langstone Ter. PL2—4G 13
Lanhydrock Rd. PL4—3B 22
Lanreath Gdns. PL2—3H 13
Lansdown Rd. PL6—1B 14
Larch Dri. PL6—2G 7
Larkham La. PL7—6H 15
Lark Hill. PL2—5E 13
Larkhill Rise. PL2—5E 13
Latham Clo. PL6—4C 14
Latimer Clo. PL7—6H 17

Latimer Wlk. PL6—2A 6
Launceston Clo. PL6—2D 6
Laurel Ct. PL2—4E 13
Laurel Dene. PL2—4E 13
Laurel Rd. PL2—4E 13
Lavington Clo. PL7—6H 17
Lawn Clo. PL7—6H 17
Lawns, The. PL2—2A 14
Lawns, The. PL11—1G 19
Lawrence Rd. PL9—1C 26
Law Wlk. PL6—3H 5
Leanway. PL12—1E 11
Leatfield Dri. PL6—4A 6
Leatherby Clo. PL6—2A 6
Leat View. PL12—6B 2
Leat Wlk. PL3—5A 14
Leat Wlk. PL6—1E 7
Leigham St. PL1—5G 21
Leigh Ct. PL6—1C 14
Leighton Rd. PL3—3A 14
Leigs Wlk. PL6—1D 6
Lester Clo. PL3—5D 14
Lewes Gdns. PL5—5G 5
Leypark Dri. PL6—1F 15
Leypark Wlk. PL6—1G 15
Liddle Way. PL7—5H 17
Lilac Clo. PL9—2E 27
Limerick Pl. PL4—4C 22
Limetree Rd. PL3—4H 13
Lincoln Av. PL4—2C 22
Linden Ter. PL4—3C 22
Linkadells. PL7—5D 16
Linketty La. PL7—6C 16
Linketty La. E. PL6—2B 14
Linketty La. W. PL3 & PL6
—3B 14
Linnet Ct. PL12—1C 10
Linton Clo. PL5—1G 5
Linton Rd. PL5—2G 5
Linton Rd. PL4—4C 22
(in two parts)
Linton Sq. PL5—2G 5
Lippell Dri. PL9—1F 27
Lipson Av. PL4—2C 22
Lipson Hill. PL4—2C 22
Lipson Rd. PL4—3A 22
(in two parts)
Lipson Ter. PL4—2C 22
Lipson Vale. PL4—1C 22
Lipstone Cres. PL4—2C 22
Liscawn Ter. PL11—3H 19
Liskeard Rd. PL12—5A 2
Lisson Gro. PL4—1A 22
Lister Clo. PL7—5F 17
Litchaton Cres. PL7—4B 16
Litchaton Way. PL7—4B 16
Litchfield Clo. PL7—5H 17
Lit. Ash Gdns. PL5—2H 11
Lit. Ash Rd. PL5—2H 11
Lit. Dock La. PL5—1E 13
Lit. Down La. PL6—1H 7
Lit. Fancy Clo. PL6—2D 6
Little La. PL9—3F 27
Littleton Pl. PL2—1D 20
Littlewood Clo. PL7—1G 25
Lizard Clo. PL6—2B 6
Lizard Wlk. PL6—2C 6
Lockington Av. PL3—4B 14
Locks Wlk. PL1—4C 20
Lockyer Ct. PL1—4H 21
Lockyer Rd. PL3—6A 14
Lockyer St. PL1—4H 21
(in two parts)
Lockyer Ter. PL12—6G 3
Lofoten Clo. PL1—3C 20
Loftus Gdns. PL5—1A 12
Longacre. PL7—4B 16
Longbridge Av. PL6—5H 15
Longbridge Clo. PL6—5H 15
Longbridge Rd. PL6—4G 15
Longbrook St. PL7—1F 25
Longcause. PL7—1F 25
Long Down Gdns. PL6—6G 7
Longfield Pl. PL4—2B 22
Longfield Vs. PL9—6F 23
Longlands La. PL12—2A 10
Longlands Rd. PL9—5F 23
Long Ley. PL3—5D 14

Longmeadow. PL7—4D 16
Longmeadow Clo. PL7—4D 16
Longmeadow Rd. PL12—6E 3
Long Pk. Clo. PL9—2H 27
Long Pk. Dri. PL6—2F 7
Long Pk. Rd. PL12—1D 10
Long Rowden. PL3—5A 14
Longstone Av. PL6—3B 6
Long Ter. Clo. PL7—6H 17
Longview Rd. PL12—6D 2
Longview Ter. PL3—4D 14
Longwood Clo. PL7—1G 25
Looe St. PL4—4A 22
Looseleigh Clo. PL6—5C 6
Looseleigh La. PL6—4A 6
Looseleigh Pk. PL6—4A 6
Lopes Rd. PL2—5F 13
Lopwell Clo. PL6—4B 6
Lorrimore Av. PL2—6D 12
Lotherton Clo. PL7—2H 25
Loughboro Rd. PL5—2A 12
Love La. PL12—1E 11
Lovell Rd. PL3—5B 14
Lwr. Compton Rd. PL3—5B 14
Lwr. Farm Rd. PL7—1G 25
Lwr. Fore St. PL12—1G 11
Lwr. Park Dri. PL9—3H 27
Lwr. Port View. PL12—1F 11
Lwr. Saltram. PL9—6E 23
Lowerside. PL2—3D 12
Lower St. PL4—4A 22
Lucas La. PL7—5D 16
Lucas Ter. PL4—3D 22
Ludlow Rd. PL3—5A 14
Lulworth Clo. PL6—2D 6
Lundy Clo. PL6—2B 6
Luscombe Clo. PL6—3H 5
Luxmore Clo. PL6—2G 15
Lych Clo. PL9—1C 26
Lydcot Wlk. PL6—3C 14
Lydford Pk. Rd. PL3—6H 13
Lympne Av. PL5—4D 4
Lyndhurst Clo. PL2—5G 13
Lyndhurst Rd. PL2—4G 13
Lyndrick Rd. PL3—4A 14
Lynher Dri. PL12—2E 11
Lynher St. PL5—1B 12
Lynmouth Clo. PL7—4C 16
Lynwood Av. PL7—5A 16

Macadam Rd. PL4—5C 22
Macaulay Cres. PL5—2G 13
Macey St. PL11—2A 20
Mackenzie Pl. PL5—1A 12
Madden Rd. PL1—3D 20
Maddock Clo. PL7—1H 25
Maddock Dri. PL7—1H 25
Madeira Rd. PL1—5H 21
Magdalen Gdns. PL7—2F 25
Maida Vale Ter. PL4—1B 22
Maidenwell Ter. PL7—5C 16
Maidstone Pl. PL5—5C 4
Maine Gdns. PL2—4D 12
Mainstone Av. PL4—4C 22
Maitland Dri. PL3—3A 14
Maker Rd. PL11—3G 19
Maker View. PL3—1F 21
Mallard Clo. PL7—6F 17
Malmesbury Clo. PL2—3F 13
Malory Clo. PL5—1H 13
Manadon Clo. PL5—2A 14
Manadon Dri. PL5—2A 14
Manby Gdns. PL5—5D 4
Manifold Gdns. PL3—6F 15
Mannamead Av. PL3—6B 14
Mannamead Ct. PL3—5B 14
Mannamead Rd. PL3—3A 14
Manor Bourne Rd. PL9—6E 27
Manor La. PL3—6F 15
Manor Pk. Clo. PL7—1F 25
Manor Pk. Dri. PL7—1F 25
Manor Rd. PL9—5G 23
Manor St. PL3—2F 21
Manston Clo. PL5—4C 4
Mantle Gdns. PL5—3B 12
Maple Av. PL11—2G 19

Maple Gro. PL4—1H 21
Maple Gro. PL7—6B 16
Maple Way. PL6—2G 7
Mardon Clo. PL6—2F 7
Marett Rd. PL5—6D 4
Margaret Pk. PL3—3A 14
Marina Rd. PL5—6D 4
Marina Ter. PL4—1A 22
Marine Dri. PL11—3H 19
Marine Pl. PL4—5B 22
Marine Rd. PL9—6D 22
Maristow Av. PL2—6D 12
Maristow Clo. PL6—4A 6
Market Av. PL1—3G 21
Market Clo. PL1—4E 21
Market Rd. PL7—6D 16
Market Sq. PL1—3G 21
Market St. PL1—4E 21
(in two parts)
Market Way. PL1—3G 21
Marlborough Clo. PL12—2F 11
Marlborough Rd. PL4—2A 22
Marlborough Row. PL1—3C 20
Marlborough St. PL1—3C 20
Marldon Clo. PL5—6F 5
Marlow Gdns. PL9—2H 27
Marrowbone Slip. PL4—4A 22
Marryat Gdns. PL5—2A 14
Marshall Rd. PL7—6A 16
Marsh Clo. PL6—5H 15
Martin La. PL4—4G 21
Martin La. PL4—4A 22
Martin St. PL1—4G 21
Martlesham Pl. PL5—5C 4
Mary Dean Av. PL5—2G 5
Mary Dean Clo. PL5—2G 5
Maryland Gdns. PL2—4D 12
Masefield Gdns. PL5—2F 13
Masterman Rd. PL2—1D 20
Maunsell Clo. PL4—4D 12
Mavisvale. PL2—5D 12
Maxwell Rd. PL4—5D 22
Maybank Rd. PL4—3C 22
Maybrook Dri. PL12—1D 10
Mayers Way. PL9—1F 27
Mayfair Cres. PL6—2D 14
Mayflower Clo. PL9—6H 23
Mayflower St. PL1—3H 21
Maynarde Clo. PL7—6H 17
May Ter. PL4—3B 22
Meadfoot Ter. PL4—6B 14
Meadow Dri. PL8—3F 29
Meadowfield Pl. PL7—2H 25
Meadowlands. PL6—2F 7
Meadow Pk. PL9—2E 27
Meadow Rise. PL7—1G 25
Meadowside. PL9—6B 24
Meadow View Rd. PL7—6C 16
Meadow Way. PL7—4D 16
Mead, The. PL7—4C 16
Meadway. PL12—2E 11
Meavy Av. PL5—1A 14
Meavy Way. PL5—1A 14
Medland Cres. PL6—3H 5
Medway Pl. PL3—5F 15
Melbourne St. PL1—2G 21
Melrose Av. PL2—3F 13
Melville Rd. PL2—4E 13
Mena Pk. Clo. PL9—6B 24
Mena Pk. Rd. PL9—6B 24
Merafield Clo. PL7—6B 16
Merafield Dri. PL7—1C 24
Merafield Rise. PL7—6C 16
Merafield Rd. PL7—1A 24
Meredith Rd. PL2—4G 13
Merlin Clo. PL6—1F 7
Merrivale Rd. PL2—4E 13
Merrivale Rd. PL6—5F 5
Mersey Clo. PL3—4F 15
Mews, The. PL1—2D 20
Michael Rd. PL3—6C 14
Michigan Way. PL3—5E 15
Mid Churchway. PL9—6A 24
Middle Down Clo. PL9—2A 28
Middlefield Pl. PL6—3H 5
Middleton Wlk. PL5—5B 4
Miers Clo. PL5—3A 12
Milch Pk. PL12—1C 10

Mildmay St. PL4—2A 22
Milehouse Rd. PL3—1E 21
Miles Mitchell Av. PL6—2C 14
Milford La. PL5—4E 5
Military Rd. PL3—5F 15
Military Rd. PL6—4E 15
Military Rd. PL11—3A 18
Millbay Rd. PL1—4E 21
Mill Bri. PL1—2F 21
Miller Ct. PL1—4F 21
Miller Way. PL6—5E 7
Mills Rd. PL1—3D 20
Millway Pl. PL9—5F 23
Millwood Dri. PL6—2G 15
Milne Pl. PL1—2C 20
Milton Clo. PL5—1G 13
Minerva Clo. PL7—5G 17
Minses Clo. PL9—6C 24
Mirador Pl. PL4—2D 22
Modbury Clo. PL6—6F 5
Modder Rd. PL11—2H 19
Molesworth Rd. PL3 & PL1
　　　　　　　—1E 21
Molesworth Rd. PL7—5B 16
Mollison Rd. PL5—1C 12
Molyneaux Pl. PL1—2D 20
Monmouth Gdns. PL5—5F 5
Montague Av. PL5—1E 13
Montgomery Clo. PL12—6D 2
Montgomery La. PL6—6C 6
Montpelier Rd. PL2—4G 13
Monument St. PL1—4C 20
Moon St. PL4—3A 22
Moorcroft Clo. PL9—6A 24
Moorfield Av. PL6—4F 7
Moorish Pk. PL9—1G 27
Moorland Av. PL7—5E 17
Moorland Dri. PL7—5E 17
Moorland Gdns. PL7—5E 17
Moorland Rd. PL6—6E 17
Moorlands La. PL12—5C 2
Moorland View. PL6—4C 6
Moorland View. PL9—6B 24
Moorland View. PL12—6F 3
Moor La. PL5—2C 12
Moor View. PL2—6D 12
Moor View. PL3—1E 23
Moor View. PL9—5F 23
Moorview Ct. PL6—4H 7
Moor View Ter. PL4—1A 22
Moreton Av. PL6—2B 14
Morice Sq. PL1—3C 20
Morice St. PL1—3C 20
Morley Clo. PL7—6A 16
Morley Ct. PL1—3G 21
Morley View Rd. PL7—5C 16
Morshead Rd. PL6—2A 14
Mortan Rd. PL12—5D 2
Mortimore Clo. PL12—1D 10
Morwell Gdns. PL2—5E 13
Moses Clo. PL6—2A 6
Mostyn Av. PL4—1C 22
Mote Pk. PL12—6C 2
Mothecombe Wlk. PL6—2G 15
Moulton Clo. PL7—1H 25
Mountbatten Clo. PL11—1F 27
Mountbatten Way. PL9—1F 27
Mt. Gould Av. PL4—3D 22
Mt. Gould Cres. PL4—2D 22
Mt. Gould Rd. PL4—2C 22
Mt. Gould Way. PL4—2D 22
Mt. Stone Rd. PL1—5E 21
Mount St. PL1—4C 20
Mount St. PL4—2A 22
Mt. Tamar Clo. PL5—1C 12
Mowhay Meadows. PL11
　　　　　　　—6B 18
Mowhay Rd. PL5—3D 12
(in two parts)
Mudge Way. PL7—6E 17
Mulberry La. PL12—1E 11
Mulby Clo. PL6—2G 7
Mullet Rd. PL3—1E 23
Mullion Clo. PL11—1F 19
Murdock Rd. PL11—2F 19
Mutley Plain. PL4—1A 22
Mutley Rd. PL3—6A 14
Mylor Clo. PL2—3H 13

Myrtle Ville. PL2—4E 13

Napier St. PL1—2D 20
Napier Ter. PL4—1A 22
Narrow La. PL12—1C 2
Nash Clo. PL7—6G 17
Neal Clo. PL7—6D 16
Neath Rd. PL4—2C 22
Nelson Av. PL1—2D 20
Nelson Gdns. PL1—2D 20
Nelson St. PL4—2A 22
Nelson St. PL11—3H 19
Nepean St. PL2—6D 12
Neswick St. PL1—3F 21
Neswick St. Ope. PL1—3F 21
Nettle Hays. PL9—6D 24
Netton Clo. PL7—2H 25
Netton Clo. PL9—1B 28
Nevada Clo. PL3—5F 15
New Barn Hill. PL7—2E 25
Newbury Clo. PL5—5F 5
Newcastle Gdns. PL5—4F 5
New George St. PL1—3G 21
Newman Rd. PL5—1C 12
Newman Rd. PL12—6F 3
Newnham Rd. PL7—4G 17
Newnham Rd. PL7—5E 17
New Pk. Rd. PL7—1G 25
New Pas. Hill. PL1—2C 20
Newport St. PL1—4E 21
New Rd. PL6—1E 7
New Rd. PL12—6D 2
New St. PL1—4A 22
Newton Av. PL5—1C 12
Newton Gdns. PL5—1D 12
New Wood Clo. PL6—1H 7
New Zealand Ho. PL3—1F 21
Nicholson Rd. PL5—1A 14
Norfolk Clo. PL6—6E 15
Norfolk Rd. PL3—6E 15
Normandy Hill. PL5—1H 11
Normandy Way. PL5—1A 12
Northampton Clo. PL6—4E 5
North Cross. PL1—2H 21
N. Down Cres. PL2—5C 12
N. Down Gdns. PL2—5D 12
N. Down Rd. PL2—5F 13
Northesk St. PL1—2E 21
North Hill. PL4—2A 22
Northolt Av. PL5—5B 4
N. Park Vs. PL12—5C 2
N. Prospect Rd. PL2—3D 12
North Rd. PL11—3G 19
North Rd. PL12—6F 3
North Rd. E. PL4—2H 21
North Rd. W. PL1—3F 21
North St. PL4—3A 22
Northumberland St. PL5—3C 12
Northumberland Ter. PL1
　　　　　　　—5G 21
N. Weald Gdns. PL5—4C 4
Norton Av. PL4—2C 22
Norwich Av. PL5—4E 5
Notte St. PL1—4H 21
Novorossisk Rd. PL6—2F 15

Oak Apple Clo. PL7—4B 16
Oakcroft Rd. PL2—4F 13
Oakdene Rise. PL9—1H 27
Oak Dri. PL6—6A 6
Oakfield Clo. PL7—5H 17
Oakfield Rd. PL4—4D 22
Oakfield St. PL7—5C 16
Oakfield Ter. Rd. PL4—4C 22
Oakham Rd. PL5—4F 5
Oaklands Clo. PL6—2E 7
Oaklands Dri. PL12—6C 2
Oaklands Grn. PL12—1C 10
Oaktree Pk. PL6—4F 7
Oakwood Clo. PL6—2F 7
Oates Rd. PL2—6F 13
Ocean Ct. PL1—5D 20
Ocean St. PL2—5C 12
Octagon St. PL1—3G 21
Octagon, The. PL1—4G 21
Okehampton Clo. PL7—1H 25

Old Ferry Rd. PL12—6F 3
Old George St. PL1—4H 21
Old Laira Rd. PL3—1C 22
Oldlands Clo. PL6—3D 6
Old Nurseries Clo. PL5—2F 5
Old Pk. Rd. PL3—5H 13
Old Priory. PL7—6D 16
Old Rd. PL8—2G 29
Old Town St. PL1—3H 21
Old Warleigh La. PL5—2E 5
Old Woodlands Rd. PL5—6G 5
Onslow Ct. PL1—4D 20
Onslow Rd. PL2—4G 13
Orchard Av. PL6—4D 14
Orchard Clo. PL7—6H 17
Orchard Cres. PL9—6E 23
Orchard Rd. PL2—4E 13
Orchardton Ter. PL9—2H 27
Orchard Vs. PL7—5D 16
Ordnance St. PL1—3B 20
Oregon Way. PL3—5E 15
Oreston Rd. PL9—6E 23
Osborne Pl. PL1—5H 21
Osborne Rd. PL3—2E 21
Osborne Vs. PL3—2E 21
Outland Rd. PL2—4F 13
Overdale Rd. PL2—4D 12
Overton Gdns. PL3—6B 14
Oxford Av. PL3—6A 14
Oxford Gdns. PL3—6A 14
Oxford Pl. PL1—3H 21
Oxford St. PL1—3G 21

Packington St. PL2—1D 20
Paddock Clo. PL9—2G 27
Palace St. PL1—4A 22
Palmerston St. PL1—2F 21
Parade. PL1—4A 22
Parade Ope. PL1—4A 22
Parade Rd. PL6—6E 5
Paradise Pl. PL1—2E 21
Paradise Rd. PL1—3D 20
Park Av. PL1—3C 20
Park Av. PL9—6F 23
Park Clo. PL7—4A 16
Park Cres. PL9—6E 23
Parker Clo. PL7—6A 16
Parker Rd. PL2—5F 13
Parkesway. PL12—1D 10
Parkfield Dri. PL6—1G 15
Park La. PL7—5G 9
Park La. PL9—6E 23
Park Pl. La. PL3—1E 21
Park Rd. PL3—5C 14
Park Rd. PL11—2H 19
Parkside. PL2—6C 12
Parkstone La. PL7—5F 17
Park St. PL3—1E 21
Park St. Ope. PL3—1E 21
Parkway, The. PL5, PL2, PL6 &
　　　　　　PL3—1B 12 to 4F 15
Parnell Clo. PL6—3C 14
Parr La. PL4—4B 22
Parr St. PL4—4B 22
Parsons Clo. PL9—2A 28
Pasley St. PL2—1C 20
Pasley St. E. PL2—1D 20
Patna Pl. PL1—2G 21
Patterdale Clo. PL6—6F 7
Patterdale Wlk. PL6—6F 7
Pattinson Clo. PL6—1G 15
Pattinson Dri. PL6—1G 15
Pawley Ct. PL12—1B 10
Paynter Wlk. PL7—6H 17
Peacock Av. PL11—2G 19
Peacock Clo. PL7—6A 16
Pearn Gdns. PL3—4C 14
Pearn Rd. PL3—5B 14
Pearson Av. PL4—1B 22
Pearson Rd. PL4—6B 14
Peeks Av. PL9—6H 23
Peel St. PL1—4E 21
Pellew Pl. PL2—1D 20
Pembrey Wlk. PL5—5C 4
Pembroke La. PL1—4C 20
Pembroke St. PL1—4D 20
Pemros Rd. PL5—1H 11

Pencair Av. PL11—3E 19
Pendeen Clo. PL6—3B 6
Pendeen Cres. PL6—3B 6
Pendennis Clo. PL3—3B 14
Pendennis Clo. PL11—2F 19
Pendilly Av. PL11—3F 19
Pengelly Clo. PL11—6F 11
Pengelly Hill. PL11—6G 11
Pengelly Pk. PL11—6F 11
Penlee Gdns. PL3—1E 21
Penlee Pk. PL11—1E 19
Penlee Pl. PL4—1B 22
Penlee Rd. PL3—1E 21
Penlee Way. PL3—1E 21
Pennycomequick Hill. PL3
　　　　　　　—2G 21
Pennycross Clo. PL2—3G 13
Pennycross Rd. PL2—4G 13
Penrith Clo. PL6—6F 7
Penrith Gdns. PL6—6F 7
Penrith Wlk. PL6—6F 7
Penrose St. PL1—2G 21
Pentamar St. PL2—1C 20
Pentillie Cres. PL4—1H 21
Pentillie Rd. PL4—1A 22
Pentland Clo. PL6—2B 6
Pentyre Ter. PL4—2B 22
Pepper La. PL9—6D 24
Pepys Pl. PL5—2H 13
Percy St. PL5—2B 12
Percy Ter. PL4—1C 22
Perranporth Clo. PL5—6C 4
Perrymans Clo. PL7—4E 17
Peter Hooper's Hill. PL5—1H 5
Peter's Clo. PL9—6B 24
Petersfield Clo. PL3—5D 14
Peter's Pk. Clo. PL5—2C 12
Peter's Pk. La. PL5—1B 12
Pethick Clo. PL6—3H 5
Pethill Clo. PL6—6H 7
Peverell Pk. Rd. PL3—4H 13
Peverell Ter. PL3—6H 13
Philip Clo. PL9—1A 28
Philip Gdns. PL9—1H 27
Phillimore St. PL2—1D 20
Phoenix St. PL1—4F 21
Pick Pie Dri. PL6—2G 7
Pier St. PL1—5G 21
Pike Rd. PL3—6F 15
Pilgrim Clo. PL2—5F 13
Pillar Wlk. PL6—2A 6
Pill La. PL12—4E 3
Pinewood Clo. PL7—5F 17
Pinewood Dri. PL6—2G 7
Pinkham Ter. PL12—3B 2
Pin La. PL1—4A 22
Plaistow Clo. PL5—1C 12
Plaistow Cres. PL5—1C 12
Pleasure Hill. PL9—5H 23
Pleasure Hill Clo. PL9—5F 23
Plough Grn. PL12—6C 2
Plumer Rd. PL6—1B 14
Plymbridge La. PL6—5D 6
Plymbridge Rd. PL6 & PL7
　　　　　　　—3E 7
Plymouth Rd. PL3, PL6 & PL7
　　　　　　—6F 15 to 6G 17
Plympton By-Pass. PL7—5H 15
　　　　　　　to 3H 25
Plympton Hill. PL7—2E 25
Plymstock Rd. PL9—6E 23
Plym St. PL4—3A 22
Plymtree Dri. PL7—4C 16
Pode Dri. PL7—1H 25
Pollard Clo. PL2—1D 26
Pollard Clo. PL12—1B 10
Polruan Ter. PL1—3F 21
Polzeath Gdns. PL2—3H 13
Pomphlett Clo. PL9—5F 23
Pomphlett Gdns. PL9—5F 23
Pomphlett Rd. PL9—5F 23
Pondfield Rd. PL12—6B 2
Ponsonby Rd. PL3—1F 21
Poole Pk. Rd. PL5—3A 12
Poplar Clo. PL7—6H 17
Porsham Clo. PL6—1D 6
Porsham La. PL5—2H 5
Porteous Clo. PL1—2C 20

Porter Way. PL12—6C 2
Portland Ct. PL1—2D 20
Portland Pl. E. PL4—2H 21
Portland Pl. PL1—2D 20
Portland Sq. PL4—2H 21
Portland Sq. La. PL4—2H 21
Portland Sq. La. N. PL4—2H 21
Portland Vs. PL4—2H 21
Port La. PL7—1E 9
Portreath Gdns. PL2—3H 13
Portway Clo. PL9—6D 24
Pottery Rd. PL1—2B 20
Poultney Clo. PL7—6G 17
Pounds Pk. PL12—6F 3
Pounds Pk. Rd. PL3—4H 13
Pound St. PL1—5E 21
Powderham Rd. PL3—4B 14
Powis Gdns. PL5—1F 13
Powisland Dri. PL6—4B 6
Pridham La. PL2—4G 13
Priestley Av. PL5—1C 12
Primrose Clo. PL11—1E 19
Prince Maurice Rd. PL4—1B 22
Princess Av. PL5—6E 5
Princess Av. PL5—1F 27
Princess Cres. PL6—1G 27
Princess St. PL1—4H 21
Princess St. Ope. PL1—4H 21
Princes St. PL1—3C 20
Princess Way. PL1—4H 21
Priors Pk. PL9—4A 24
Priory Dri. PL7—6D 16
Priory Lawn Ter. PL3—5C 14
Priory Mill. PL7—6D 16
Priory Ridge. PL7—6D 16
Priory Rd. PL3—5C 14
Promenade, The. PL1—5H 21
Prospect Pl. PL1—4G 21
Prospect Row. PL1—4C 20
Prospect St. PL4—3A 22
Prospect Wlk. PL12—6C 2
Prouse Cres. PL2—3G 13
Prouse Rise. PL12—1E 11
Providence Pl. PL1—2E 21
Providence St. PL4—2A 22
Prynne Clo. PL1—3G 21
Pym St. PL1—2D 20
Pyne Vs. PL9—1D 26

Quarry Pk. Av. PL9—6F 23
Quarry Pk. Rd. PL3—6H 13
Quarry Pk. Rd. PL9—6F 23
Quarry St. PL11—2H 19
Quarterdeck, The. PL1—5E 21
Quay Rd. PL4—4A 22
Quay, The. PL9—5E 23
Queen Anne Pl. PL4—5B 22
Queen's Ga. PL1—2F 21
Queen's Ga. PL4—2B 22
Queen's Ga. M. PL4—2B 22
Queen's Ga. Vs. PL4—2B 22
Queen's Rd. PL4—2B 22
Queen Rd. PL5—6D 4
Queen St. PL1—3B 20

Radcliffe Clo. PL6—2A 6
Radford Av. PL4—4C 22
Radford Pk. Dri. PL9—1F 27
Radford Pk. Rd. PL9—1F 27
Radford Rd. PL1—5G 21
Radford View. PL9—1F 27
Radnor Pl. PL4—3A 22
Radnor St. PL4—3A 22
Raglan Ct. PL1—4D 20
Raglan Gdns. PL1—3D 20
Raglan Rd. PL1—3D 20
Railway Cotts. PL12—6D 12
Raleigh Ct. PL7—5H 17
Raleigh St. PL1—3G 21
Ramage Clo. PL6—6H 7
Ramillies Av. PL5—5E 5
Randwick Pk. Rd. PL9—6F 23
Raphael Clo. PL9—1A 28
Raphael Dri. PL9—1A 28
Rashleigh Av. PL7—4E 17
Rashleigh Av. PL12—2D 10

Rawlin Clo. PL6—3E 15
Raymond Way. PL7—5D 16
Raynham Rd. PL3—2F 21
Reading Wlk. PL5—5G 5
Recreation Rd. PL6—4C 6
Rectory Rd. PL1—3E 21
Reddicliff Clo. PL9—2E 27
Reddicliff Rd. PL9—2E 27
Reddington Rd. PL3—4D 14
Redhill Clo. PL5—5C 4
Red Lion Hill. PL6—1G 29
Redruth Clo. PL5—2G 5
Redwing Dri. PL6—1F 7
Redwood Dri. PL7—6E 17
Regent St. PL4—3A 22
Reigate Rd. PL9—5G 23
Rendlesham Gdns. PL6—6G 7
Rendlesham Rd. PL6—6G 7
Rendle St. PL1—3F 21
Rennie Av. PL5—2A 12
Renny Rd. PL6—6E 27
Renoir Clo. PL9—1A 28
Renown St. PL2—5C 12
Reservoir Cres. PL9—6B 24
Reservoir La. PL3—5B 14
Reservoir Rd. PL3—5B 14
Reservoir Rd. PL9—1B 28
Reservoir Way. PL9—6B 24
Restormel Rd. PL4—5B 14
Retreat, The. PL3—4D 14
Revell Pk. Rd. PL7—5D 16
Revel Rd. PL3—5C 14
Reynolds Gro. PL5—3A 12
Reynolds Wood. PL7—4C 16
Rheola Gdns. PL6—5F 7
Rhodes Clo. PL7—1H 5
Ribble Gdns. PL3—4F 15
Richmond Rd. PL6—1H 14
Richmond Wlk. PL1—4C 20
Ride, The. PL9—4E 23
Ridge Pk. PL7—6E 17
Ridge Pk. Av. PL4—1H 21
Ridge Pk. Rd. PL7—6E 17
Ridge Rd. PL7—2F 25
(in two parts)
Ridgeway. PL7—6D 16
Ridgeway. PL2—2D 10
Riga Ter. PL3—6E 15
Rigdale Clo. PL6—3C 14
Ringmore Way. PL5—5E 5
Risdon Av. PL4—4D 22
Riverford Clo. PL6—2F 7
Riverside Pl. PL1—3B 20
Riverside Wlk. PL1—3F 5
Rivers, The. PL12—2E 11
River View. PL4—4C 22
River View La. PL4—4C 22
Robert Adams Clo. PL7—6A 16
Roberts Av. PL11—2G 19
Roberts Rd. PL5—3A 12
Roborough Av. PL6—4D 6
Roborough Clo. PL6—4D 6
Roborough La. PL5—1G 5
Robyns Clo. PL7—6H 17
Rochester Rd. PL4—1A 22
Rochford Cres. PL5—4D 4
Rockfield Av. PL6—3A 6
Rock Gdns. PL9—4F 23
Rock Hill. PL5—3G 5
Rockingham Rd. PL3—6C 14
Rockville Rd. PL9—5G 23
Rockwood Rd. PL6—1G 7
Rocky Pk. Av. PL9—5F 23
Rocky Pk. Rd. PL9—6G 23
Roddick Way. PL7—6H 17
Rodney St. PL5—3B 12
Roeslare Av. PL11—2G 19
Roeslare Clo. PL11—2G 19
Rogate Dri. PL6—5E 7
Rogate Wlk. PL6—5E 7
Rollis Pk. Clo. PL9—6E 23
Rollis Pk. Rd. PL9—5E 23
Rolston Clo. PL3—6H 5
Roman Rd. PL5—2C 12
Roman Way. PL5—1C 12
Roman Way. PL6—2G 7
Romilly Gdns. PL7—6A 16
Ronald Ter. PL2—6D 12

Ronsdale Clo. PL9—5F 23
Roope Clo. PL5—4A 12
Roper Av. PL9—5F 23
Rosebery La. PL4—2C 22
Rosebery Rd. PL4—2C 22
Rosebury Av. PL4—2C 22
Roseclave Clo. PL7—6H 17
Rose Cotts. PL6—3D 14
Rosedale Clo. PL2—4G 13
Rosedown Av. PL2—4E 13
Rose Gdns. PL6—3F 7
Rosehip Clo. PL6—2G 7
Rosevean Ct. PL3—5B 14
Rosevean Gdns. PL3—5B 14
Roseveare Clo. PL9—5A 24
Rosewood Clo. PL9—2H 27
Rospeath Cres. PL2—3H 13
Rosslyn Pk. Rd. PL3—6H 13
Ross St. PL2—1C 20
(in two parts)
Rothbury Clo. PL6—5G 7
Rothbury Gdns. PL6—5G 7
Rothesay Gdns. PL5—5G 5
Rougemont Clo. PL3—4D 14
Rowan Clo. PL7—6H 17
Rowden St. PL3—6A 14
Rowen Ct. PL12—1C 10
Rowe St. PL4—3H 21
Rowe St. PL11—2H 19
Rowland Clo. PL9—2G 27
Row La. PL5—1C 12
Royal Pde. PL1—4H 21
Royal William Rd. PL1—5E 21
Rudyard Wlk. PL3—5E 15
Rufford Clo. PL2—4E 13
Ruskin Cres. PL5—1H 13
Russell Av. PL3—4A 14
Russell Clo. PL9—5B 24
Russell Clo. PL12—6C 2
Russell Pl. PL3—2H 21
Rutger Pl. PL1—2F 21
Ruthven Clo. PL6—3B 14
Rutland Rd. PL4—1B 22
Rydal Clo. PL6—1F 15
Ryder Rd. PL2—1D 20
(in two parts)
Rye Hill. PL12—1C 10

St Andrew Pl. PL1—4H 21
St Andrew's Clo. PL12—1C 10
St Andrew's Cross. PL1—4H 21
St Andrew St. PL1—4H 21
St Anne's Rd. PL6—3F 5
St Anne's Rd. PL12—6E 3
St Aubyn Av. PL2—6D 12
St Aubyn Rd. PL1—2C 20
St Barnabas Ter. PL1—2F 21
St Boniface Clo. PL2—4G 13
St Boniface Dri. PL2—4G 13
St Bridget Av. PL6—2B 14
St Budeaux By-Pass. PL5
—3C 12
St Dunstan's Ter. PL4—3C 22
St Edwards Gdns. PL6—2D 14
St Elizabeth Clo. PL7—1F 25
St Erth Rd. PL2—3H 13
St Eval Pl. PL5—5C 4
St Francis Ct. PL5—6E 5
St Gabriel's Av. PL3—6H 13
St Georges Av. PL2—4G 13
St George's Rd. PL12—6D 2
St George's Ter. PL2—1D 20
St Helen's Wlk. PL5—5G 5
St Hilary Ter. PL4—3C 22
St James Pl. E. PL1—4G 21
St James Pl. W. PL1—4G 21
St James Rd. PL11—2H 19
St John's Bri. PL4—4B 22
St John's Clo. PL6—4F 7
St Johns Dri. PL9—1D 26
St John's Rd. PL4—4B 22
St John's Rd. PL9—1C 26
St John's St. PL4—4B 22
St Joseph's Clo. PL6—2B 14
St Judes Rd. PL4—4B 22
St Keverne Pl. PL2—3H 13

St Lawrence Rd. PL4—2A 22
St Leonards Rd. PL4—4C 22
St Leo Pl. PL2—1C 20
St Levan Rd. PL2—6C 12
St Margarets Rd. PL7—4A 16
St Marks Rd. PL6—4E 7
St Martin's Av. PL3—4H 13
St Mary's Clo. PL7—6C 16
St Mary's Ct. PL7—5B 16
St Mary's Rd. PL7—5B 16
St Mary St. PL1—3F 21
St Maurice M. PL7—1E 25
St Maurice Rd. PL7—2F 25
St Maurice View. PL7—1H 25
St Mawes Ter. PL2—6D 12
St Micheal Av. PL2—6D 12
St Micheal's Clo. PL1—4C 20
St Micheal's Ter. PL1—2D 20
St Modwen Rd. PL6—4G 15
St Nazaire App. PL1—3C 20
St Nazaire Clo. PL1—3C 20
St Pancras Av. PL2—2G 13
St Paul's Clo. PL3—6E 15
St Paul St. PL1—5F 21
St Peter Clo. PL7—1F 25
St Peters Rd. PL5—1G 13
St Stephen's Hill. PL12—2C 10
St Stephens Rd. PL7—2F 25
St Stephen's Rd. PL12—2D 10
St Stephen's Wlk. PL7—1D 40
St Thomas Clo. PL7—2F 25
St Vincent St. PL2—1C 20
Salamanca St. PL11—2H 19
Salcombe Rd. PL4—1B 22
Salisbury Rd. PL4—3B 22
Salisbury Ter. PL3—1E 21
Saltash By-Pass. PL12—5B 2
Saltash Rd. PL2—6B 12
Saltburn Rd. PL5—2A 12
Saltmill. PL12—5F 3
Saltram Ter. PL7—6D 16
Sandon Wlk. PL6—3C 14
Sandy La. PL7—1H 25
Sanford Rd. PL9—5H 23
Sango Rd. PL11—3G 19
Sarum Rd. PL3—4B 14
Saunders Wlk. PL6—3G 5
Savage Rd. PL5—4A 12
Sawrey St. PL1—4F 21
School Clo. PL7—4D 16
School La. PL7—1E 25
Sconner Rd. PL11—2G 19
Scott Av. PL5—3A 12
Scott Rd. PL2—6F 13
Seacroft Rd. PL5—1A 12
Seaton Av. PL4—1A 22
Seaton La. PL4—1A 22
Seaton Pl. PL2—6D 12
Seaview Av. PL4—2C 22
Sea View Ter. PL4—2B 22
Second Av. PL1—3E 21
Second Av. PL4—4C 12
Second Av. PL9—4H 23
Sefton Av. PL4—1C 22
Sefton Clo. PL4—2C 22
Segrave Rd. PL2—6F 13
Selkirk Pl. PL5—1A 14
Sellon Ct. PL1—3G 21
Selsden Clo. PL9—1B 28
Sennen Clo. PL11—1F 19
Serpell Clo. PL6—3A 6
Seven Stars La. PL5—3F 5
Severn Pl. PL3—6E 15
Seymour Av. PL4—2B 22
Seymour Dri. PL3—6B 14
Seymour M. PL4—2B 22
Seymour Rd. PL3—6B 14
Seymour Rd. PL4—2B 22
Seymour Rd. PL7—5B 16
Seymour St. PL4—3A 22
Shaftesbury Cotts. PL4—2A 22
Shaftesbury Ct. PL4—2A 22
Shakespeare Rd. PL5—1F 13
Shaldon Cres. PL5—6F 5
Shallowford Clo. PL6—3E 15
Shallowford Rd. PL6—4E 15
Shapleys Gdns. PL9—2A 28
Shapters Way. PL4—4C 22

Sharon Way. PL6—4C 6
Sharrose Rd. PL9—2D 26
Shearwood Clo. PL7—5C 16
Sheepstor Rd. PL6—2F 15
Shell Clo. PL6—2G 15
Shelley Way. PL5—2B 12
Shepherds La. PL4—4B 22
Sherborne Clo. PL9—1C 28
Sherford Cres. PL5—6D 4
Sherford Cres. PL9—6C 24
Sherford Rd. PL9—6C 24
Sheridan Rd. PL5—2A 12
Sherril Clo. PL9—3H 27
Sherwell La. PL4—2H 21
Shipley Wlk. PL6—2C 14
Shirburn Rd. PL3—3D 14
Shirley Gdns. PL5—2G 13
Short Pk. Rd. PL3—6H 13
Shortwood Cres. PL9—5A 24
Shrewsbury Rd. PL5—5F 5
Shute Pk. Rd. PL9—1H 27
Silver Birch Clo. PL6—2E 7
Silver Birch Rd. PL7—6H 17
Silver St. PL12—1G 11
Simon Clo. PL9—1G 27
Sithney St. PL5—2A 12
Six O'Clock La. PL7—2E 25
Skardale Gdns. PL6—3F 15
Skardon Pl. PL4—2A 22
Skerries Rd. PL6—3B 6
Skylark Rise. PL6—1G 7
Slade Clo. PL9—2A 28
Slatelands Clo. PL7—2H 25
Sleep Clo. PL12—6B 2
Smallack Clo. PL6—1B 14
Smallack Dri. PL6—1B 14
Smallridge Clo. PL9—2H 27
Smeaton Sq. PL3—5F 15
Smithfield Dri. PL12—6B 2
Smiths Way. PL12—6B 2
Smithy Clo. PL12—5C 2
Snell Dri. PL12—6B 2
Somerset Cotts. PL3—1E 21
Somerset Pl. PL3—1E 21
Sopers Hill. PL5—1A 6
S. Down Rd. PL2—5F 13
Southdown Ter. PL10—6G 19
Southern Clo. PL2—4C 12
Southern Ter. PL4—1B 22
Southernway. PL9—6A 24
Southfield. PL12—6C 2
Southgate Av. PL6—2G 27
Southgate Clo. PL9—2G 27
South Hill. PL1—2E 21
South Hill. PL9—2E 27
S. Milton St. PL4—4C 22
Southside Ope. PL1—4A 22
Southside St. PL1—4A 22
South View. PL5—1A 14
South View. PL9—6B 24
S. View Clo. PL7—4D 16
S. View Pk. PL7—4D 16
S. View Ter. PL7—3C 22
Southway Dri. PL6—4H 5
Southway La. PL6—2D 6
Southwell Rd. PL6—2A 14
Sparke Clo. PL7—1H 25
Spears, The. PL7—1B 10
Speedwell Cres. PL6—4C 14
Speedwell Wlk. PL6—4D 14
Spencer Gdns. PL12—2E 11
Spencer Rd. PL9—5G 23
Spinney, The. PL7—1G 25
Spire Hill Pk. PL12—1C 10
Spring Bank. PL6—2G 7
Springfield Av. PL9—6A 24
Springfield Clo. PL9—6A 24
Springfield La. PL6—6A 24
Springfield Rise. PL9—6B 24
Springfield Rd. PL9—1A 28
Springhill. PL2—3G 13
Springhill Grn. PL2—3G 13
Springwood Clo. PL7—2G 25
Spruce Gdns. PL7—6H 17
Square, The. PL1—3F 21

Square, The. PL12—6C 2
Staddiscombe Rd. PL9—4H 27
Staddon Cres. PL9—1G 27
Staddon Grn. PL9—1F 27
Staddon La. PL9—3D 26
Staddon Pk. Rd. PL9—1G 27
Stag La. PL9—5B 24
(in two parts)
Stamford Clo. PL9—1C 26
Stanborough Cross. PL9—6C 24
Stanborough Rd. PL9—6H 23
Stanbury Av. PL6—1A 14
Standarhay Vs. PL9—6C 24
Stangray Av. PL4—1H 21
Stanhope Rd. PL5—1A 12
Stanlake Clo. PL12—1D 10
Stanley Pl. PL4—3D 22
Staple Clo. PL6—1F 7
Stapleford Gdns. PL5—4D 4
Station Rd. PL2—6C 12
Station Rd. PL7—5D 16
Station Rd. PL9—6C 24
Station Rd. PL12—1G 11
Steeple Clo. PL9—3H 27
Steer Pk. Rd. PL7—6H 17
Steer Point Rd. PL8—2G 29
Stefan Clo. PL9—2D 26
Stenlake Pl. PL4—3D 22
Stenlake Ter. PL4—3D 22
Stentaway Clo. PL9—5H 23
Stentaway Dri. PL9—5H 23
Stentaway Rd. PL9—6H 23
Stephenson Way. PL5—1D 12
Stillman St. PL4—4A 22
Stirling Rd. PL5—2A 12
Stoggy La. PL7—5H 17
(in two parts)
Stoke Rd. PL3—2F 21
Stokes La. PL1—4A 22
Stokingway Clo. PL9—2G 27
Stone Barton Clo. PL7—5C 16
Stone Barton Rd. PL7—5C 16
Stonehouse St. PL1—4E 21
Stopford Pl. PL1—2D 20
Stott Clo. PL3—6F 15
Stour Clo. PL3—5G 15
Stowe Gdns. PL5—1F 13
Strand St. PL1—5E 21
Straton Wlk. PL2—3H 13
Strode Rd. PL7—4E 17
Stroma Clo. PL6—2B 6
Stroud Pk. Rd. PL3—4G 13
Stuart Rd. PL1 & PL3—2E 21
Sturdee Rd. PL2—6E 13
Summerfields. PL12—2C 10
Summers Clo. PL6—4D 14
Sunderland Clo. PL9—1C 26
Sunningdale Rd. PL12—1C 10
Sunny Banks. PL12—1A 2
Sunny Dene. PL5—2B 12
Sunnyside Rd. PL4—3D 22
Sunwell La. PL11—5A 18
Sussex Pl. PL4—1H 21
Sussex Rd. PL2—6D 12
Sussex St. PL1—4H 21
Sussex Ter. PL2—6D 12
Sutherland Rd. PL4—1H 21
Sutton Rd. PL4—4B 22
Swaindale Rd. PL3—5A 14
Swale Clo. PL3—5D 14
Swallow Rd. PL2—6B 2
Swan Gdns. PL7—6H 17
Swift Gdns. PL5—1G 13
Swinborne Gdns. PL5—2F 13
Sycamore Av. PL4—5C 22
Sycamore Dri. PL6—2E 7
Sycamore Dri. PL7—2F 19
Sycamore Way. PL6—3G 7
Sydney Clo. PL7—1E 25
Sydney Rd. PL11—2G 19
Sydney St. PL1—2G 21
Symons Rd. PL12—1F 11

Tailyour Rd. PL6—1B 14
Talbot Gdns. PL5—4A 12
Tamar Av. PL2—6C 12

Tamar Bri. Rd. PL5—1A 12
Tamar Bri. PL12 & PL5—1G 11
Tamar St. PL1—2C 20
Tamar St. PL12—1G 11
Tamar Vs. PL9—6F 23
Tamar Wharf. PL1—2B 20
Tamerton Av. PL5—4C 4
Tamerton Clo. PL5—3E 5
Tamerton Foliot Rd. PL5 & PL6
—3G 5
Tangmere Av. PL5—4C 4
Tapps La. PL8—2H 29
Tapson Dri. PL9—1C 26
Taunton Av. PL5—4F 5
Taunton Pl. PL5—4F 5
Tavistock Old Rd. PL3—3A 14
Tavistock Pl. PL4—3A 22
Tavistock Rd. PL5 & PL6
—3A 14 to 1E 7
Tavy Pl. PL4—1B 22
Tavy Rd. PL12—6G 3
Taw Clo. PL3—5G 15
Tay Gdns. PL3—4F 15
Taylor Clo. PL12—6C 2
Taylor Rd. PL12—6C 2
Teats Hill Rd. PL4—4B 22
Tees Gdns. PL3—4E 15
Teign Rd. PL3—5D 14
Telford Cres. PL5—1D 12
Tenby Rd. PL5—2A 12
Tennyson Gdns. PL5—2F 13
Tern Gdns. PL7—6F 17
Terrace, The. PL1—3B 20
Terra Nova Gro. PL2—6F 13
Tewkesbury Clo. PL2—3E 13
Thackeray Gdns. PL5—2F 13
Thames Gdns. PL3—5F 15
Thanckes Dri. PL11—1G 19
Theatre Ope. PL1—4D 20
Therlow Rd. PL3—5D 14
Thetford Gdns. PL6—3F 15
Third Av. PL1—3E 21
Third Av. PL2—4C 12
Third Av. PL9—4A 24
Thirlmere Gdns. PL6—5B 6
Thistle Clo. PL6—2G 7
Thistle Pk. Rd. PL4—4B 22
Thornbury Pk. Av. PL3—5H 13
Thornbury Rd. PL6—5G 7
Thornhill Rd. PL3—5A 14
Thornhill Way. PL3—5A 14
Thorn La. PL12—6C 2
Thorn Pk. PL3—6A 14
Thornton Av. PL4—2B 22
Thornyville Dri. PL9—5E 23
Thornyville Dri. PL9—6E 23
Thornyville Ter. PL9—6E 23
Thornyville Vs. PL9—6E 23
Thurlestone Wlk. PL6—2F 15
Tillard Clo. PL7—6H 17
Tilly Clo. PL9—3H 27
Tincombe. PL12—1C 10
Tin La. PL4—4A 22
Tintagle Cres. PL2—3G 13
Tintern Av. PL4—4C 22
Tithe Rd. PL7—4A 16
Tiverton Clo. PL6—1D 6
Tobruk Rd. PL12—6E 3
Tollox Pl. PL3—1D 22
Torbridge Clo. PL12—1D 10
Torbridge Rd. PL7—5E 17
Torbryan Clo. PL6—3G 15
Tor Clo. PL3—4A 14
Tor Cres. PL3—4A 14
Torland Rd. PL3—4A 14
Tor La. PL3—4H 13
Torridge Clo. PL7—5F 17
Torridge Rd. PL7—5F 17
Torridge Way. PL3—6E 15
Tor Rd. PL3—4A 14
Torr View Av. PL3—4H 13
Torver Clo. PL6—1F 15
Tory Brook Av. PL7—5E 17
Tory Brook Ct. PL7—5E 17
Tory Way. PL7—5D 16
Tothill Av. PL4—3B 22
Tothill Pl. PL4—3B 22
Totnes Clo. PL7—1H 25

Tower Ct. PL12—1C 10
Towers Clo. PL6—6H 7
Tower View. PL12—2D 10
Towns End. PL12—6B 2
Townshend Av. PL2—6C 12
Tracey Ct. PL1—3G 21
Trafalgar Pl. La. PL1—2D 20
Trafalgar St. PL4—3A 22
Train Rd. PL9—6B 28
Tramway Rd. PL6—2F 7
Transit Way. PL5—6G 5
Treago Gdns. PL6—1D 6
Treby Rd. PL7—1F 25
Trefusis Gdns. PL3—6C 14
Tregenna Clo. PL7—1H 25
Tregoning Rd. PL11—3F 19
Trelawney Clo. PL11—2E 19
Trelawney Rise PL11—2E 19
Trelawney Rd. PL3—6H 13
Trelawney Rd. PL12—1E 11
Trelawney Rd. La. PL3—6H 13
Trelawney Way. PL11—2E 19
Trelawny Av. PL5—2B 12
Trelawny Pl. PL5—2B 12
Trelawny Rd. PL7—4C 16
Treloweth Clo. PL2—3H 13
Trematon Clo. PL11—1E 19
Trematon Ter. PL4—1A 22
Trendwood Rd. PL6—2F 7
Trengrouse Av. PL11—2F 19
Trent Clo. PL3—5D 14
Trentham Clo. PL6—3C 6
Tresillian Av. PL4—4C 22
Tresluggan Rd. PL5—2B 12
Tretower Clo. PL6—4B 6
Trevannion Clo. PL6—3C 6
Treveneague Gdns. PL2—3H 13
Treverbyn Rd. PL7—5D 16
Trevessa Clo. PL2—3H 13
Trevithick Av. PL11—1E 19
Trevithick Rd. PL5—2C 12
Trevol Pl. PL11—2E 19
(in two parts)
Trevol Rd. PL11—2C 18
Trevone Gdns. PL2—3H 13
Trevorder Clo. PL11—3F 19
Trevorder Rd. PL11—3F 19
Trowbridge Clo. PL5—5G 5
Truro Dri. PL5—4E 5
Tucker Clo. PL5—3D 12
Tudor Clo. PL9—2G 27
Turbill Gdns. PL7—6H 17
Turret Gro. PL4—1B 22
Tuxton Clo. PL7—2H 25
Two Hills Pk. PL12—1C 10
Tylney Clo. PL3—6D 6
Tyndale Clo. PL5—2F 13
Tything Wlk. PL3—5A 14

Ullswater Cres. PL6—4A 6
Undercliff Rd. PL6—6H 7
Underhill Rd. PL3—1E 21
Underhill Vs. PL3—2E 21
Underlane. PL7—6B 16
Underlane. PL9—1F 27
Underwood Rd. PL7—6D 16
Union Pl. PL1—4F 21
Union St. PL1—4F 21
Unity Clo. PL6—4G 7
Upland Dri. PL6—4B 6
Uplands. PL12—2E 11
Upton Clo. PL3—4D 14
Uxbridge Dri. PL5—5C 4

Vaagso Clo. PL1—3C 20
Valiant Av. PL5—5D 4
Vallard's La. PL12—1A 2
Valletort Pl. PL1—3E 21
Valletort Rd. PL1—2E 21
Valley Rd. PL12—1E 11
Valley Rd. La. PL6—1B 6
Valley View. PL6—2F 7
Valley View Clo. PL3—4D 14
Valley View Rd. PL3—4D 14
Vapron Rd. PL3—4D 14
Vauban Pl. PL2—1D 20
Vaughan Clo. PL2—4G 13
Vauxhall St. PL1 & PL4—4A 22

Vauxhall St. Flats. PL4—4A 22
Venn Clo. PL3—5A 14
Venn Ct. PL3—5A 14
Venn Cres. PL3—5A 14
Venn Dri. PL8—3F 29
Venn Gdns. PL3—4A 14
Venn Gro. PL3—4A 14
Venn La. PL2 & PL3—5G 13
Venn Way. PL3—4A 14
Vermont Gdns. PL2—4D 12
Verna Pl. PL5—1B 12
Verna Rd. PL5—1B 12
Vicarage Gdns. PL5—2H 11
Vicarage Rd. PL7—5C 16
Vicarage Rd. PL11—3H 19
Victoria Av. PL1—2F 21
Victoria Cotts. PL6—3D 14
Victoria Pl. PL2—1D 20
Victoria St. PL2—2B 12
Victoria Rd. PL3—6H 13
Victoria Rd. PL11—2H 19
Victory St. PL2—5C 12
Villiers Clo. PL9—6F 23
Vincent Way. PL12—1F 11
Vine Cres. PL2—5F 13
Vine Gdns. PL2—5F 13
Vinery La. PL9 & PL7—6D 24
Vinstone Way. PL5—2B 12
Violet Dri. PL6—1G 7
Virginia Gdns. PL2—4D 12

Waddon Clo. PL7—4E 17
Wadham Ter. PL2—6D 12
Waggon Hill. PL7—1G 25
Wain Pk. PL7—1F 25
Wakefield Av. PL5—2B 12
Wake St. PL3—2G 21
Walcot Clo. PL6—6G 7
Waldon Clo. PL7—5H 17
Walker Ter. PL1—5G 21
Walkhampton Wlk. PL6—2F 15
Wallace Rd. PL7—1G 25
Wall Pk. Clo. PL7—4F 17
Walnut Clo. PL7—6H 17
Walnut Dri. PL7—6H 17
Walsingham Ct. PL7—5H 17
Walters Rd. PL5—1A 12
Waltham Pl. PL2—3E 13
Walton Cres. PL5—2G 13
Wandle Pl. PL3—6F 15
Wanstead Gro. PL5—6E 5
Warburton Gdns. PL5—2H 11
Wardlow Clo. PL6—3B 14
Wardlow Gdns. PL6—3B 14
Wardour Wlk. PL6—1D 6
Ward Pl. PL3—6D 14
Warfelton Cres. PL12—1E 11
Waring Rd. PL6—2H 5
Warleigh Av. PL2—6C 12
Warleigh Cres. PL6—4A 6
Warleigh La. PL2—6C 12
Warleigh Rd. PL4—1A 22
Warmwell Rd. PL5—5C 4
Warraton Clo. PL12—6D 2
Warraton Grn. PL12—6D 2
Warraton La. PL12—6D 2
Warraton Rd. PL12—6D 2
Warren La. PL5—1E 5
Warren Pk. PL6—2F 7
Warren St. PL2—1C 20
Warwick Av. PL5—6G 5
Warwick Orchard Clo. PL5
—6F 5
Wasdale Clo. PL6—1F 15
Wasdale Gdns. PL6—1F 15
Washbourne Clo. PL1—2C 20
Waterloo Clo. PL1—3E 21
Waterloo Ct. PL1—3E 21
Waterloo St. PL1—2D 20
Waterloo St. PL4—2A 22
Watson Gdns. PL4—4B 22
Watson Rd. PL4—3B 22
Watts Pk. Rd. PL2—4G 13
Watts Rd. PL4—3C 22
Waveney Gdns. PL6—6G 5
Waverley Rd. PL5—1B 12
Wavish Pk. PL11—2E 19
Waycott Wlk. PL6—3G 5

Wearde Rd. PL12—1D 10
Weir Clo. PL6—6H 7
Weir Gdns. PL6—1H 15
Weir Rd. PL6—6H 7
Welbeck Av. PL4—4H 21
Welland Gdns. PL3—6E 15
Wellfield Clo. PL7—6H 17
Well Gdns. PL1—3G 21
Wellhay Clo. PL9—1C 28
Wellington St. PL1—2E 21
Wellington St. PL4—2A 22
Wellington St. PL11—3H 19
Well Pk. Rd. PL11—2H 19
Wellsbourne Pk. PL3—5C 14
Welsford Av. PL2—6D 12
Wembury Pk. Rd. PL3—5H 13
Wembury Rd. PL9—2A 28
Wenlock Gdns. PL2—3F 13
Wensum Clo. PL7—6G 17
Wentwood Gdns. PL6—6G 7
Wentwood Pl. PL6—5G 7
Wentworth Pl. PL4—3C 22
Wesley Av. PL3—6A 14
Wesley Pl. PL2—1D 20
Wesley Pl. PL3—6A 14
Wesley Rd. PL12—1F 11
Westbourne Rd. PL3—6H 13
Westbourne Ter. PL12—6F 3
Westcombe Cres. PL9—2E 27
Westcott Clo. PL6—4C 14
Westcountry Clo. PL2—4D 12
Westcroft Rd. PL5—2B 12
W. Down Rd. PL2—5E 13
Westeria Ter. PL2—4C 12
Western App. PL1—4G 21
Western College Rd. PL4—6A 14
Western Dri. PL3—1D 22
Westfield. PL7—5F 17
Westfield Av. PL9—1E 27
Westhampnett Pl. PL5—4D 4
Westhays Clo. PL3—4H 27
W. Hill Rd. PL4—1B 22
W. Hoe Rd. PL1—4G 21
Westlake Clo. PL11—2F 19
W. Malling Av. PL5—4C 4
Westmoor Clo. PL7—5H 17
Weston Mill Dri. PL5—4C 12
Weston Mill Hill. PL5—2D 12
Weston Mill La. PL5—2E 13
Weston Mill Rd. PL5—2C 12
Weston Pk. Rd. PL3—4H 13
Weston Pk. Rd. PL7—6H 17
W. Park Hill. PL7—4G 17
Westway. PL9—1D 26
Westwood Av. PL6—3E 7
Wheatridge. PL7—4B 16
Whimple St. PL1—4H 21
Whin Bank Rd. PL5—1H 13
Whitby Cres. PL6—2C 14
Whitby Rd. PL6—2C 14
Whitefield Ter. PL4—2B 22
Whiteford Rd. PL3—5A 14
Whitehall Dri. PL6—8B 24
White La. PL1—4A 22
Whitleigh Av. PL5—1A 14
Whitleigh Grn. PL5—5G 5
Whitleigh Vs. PL5—1A 14
Whitleigh Way. PL5—5G 5
(in two parts)
Whitsoncross La. PL5—2G 5
Whittington St. PL3—2F 21
Widewell La. PL6—2G 7
Widewell Rd. PL6—3D 6
Widey La. PL6—2G 7
Widey View. PL3—4B 14
Wilbert Rd. PL6—3F 15
Wilcove La. PL11—6E 11
Wilderness Rd. PL3—6A 14
Wilkinson Rd. PL5—4A 12
Williams Av. PL4—4D 22
Willow Clo. PL3—6G 15
Willow Ct. PL6—4G 15
Willow Grn. PL12—1D 10
Willow Wlk. PL6—4F 7
Wills Clo. PL6—2A 6
Wilson Cres. PL2—6F 13
Wilton Rd. PL1—2E 21
Wilton St. PL1—2F 21

Winchester Gdns. PL5—4E 5
Windermere Cres. PL6—5B 6
Windmill Hill. PL12—1E 11
Windsor La. PL12—1E 11
Windsor Pl. PL1—4H 21
Windsor Rd. PL3—4D 14
Wingfield Rd. PL2—2G 21
Wingfield Way. PL3—2F 21
Winnicott Clo. PL6—2A 6
Winnow Clo. PL9—3G 27
Winsbury Ct. PL6—2B 14
Winstanley Wlk. PL3—5F 15
Winston Av. PL4—2H 21
Winstone La. PL8—2H 29
Witham Gdns. PL3—6E 15
Withnoe La. PL11—6B 18
Woburn Ter. PL9—6E 23
Wollaton Gro. PL5—6D 4
Wolridge Av. PL7—6G 17
Wolridge Way. PL7—6G 17
Wolsdon Pl. PL1—3F 21
Wolsdon St. PL1—3F 21
Wolseley Rd. PL5 & PL2—2B 12
Wolverwood Clo. PL7—2H 25
Wolverwood La. PL7—2F 25
Wombwell Cres. PL2—4C 12
Woodbury Gdns. PL5—6E 5
Wood Clo. PL12—6B 2
Woodend Rd. PL6—2F 7
Woodford Av. PL7—4A 16
Woodford Clo. PL7—4A 16
Woodford Cres. PL7—5A 16
Woodford Grn. PL7—5B 16
Woodford Rd. PL6—3F 7
Woodhey Rd. PL2—4E 13
Woodland Av. PL9—5A 24
Woodland Dri. PL8—1B 24
Woodland Rd. PL7—5C 16
Woodlands. PL9—1H 27
Woodlands Ct. PL5—6E 5
Woodlands La. PL6—1H 15
Woodland Ter. PL4—2B 22
Woodland Way. PL11—2F 19
Woodside. PL4—2B 22
Woodside Av. PL9—2E 27
Woodstock Gdns. PL5—2A 12
Woodview Pk. PL9—1A 28
Woodville Rd. PL2—4D 12
Woodway. PL9—6A 24
Woolcombe Av. PL7—1F 25
Woolwell Cres. PL6—1E 7
Woolwell Dri. PL6—2E 7
Woolwell Rd. PL6—2E 7
Wordsworth Cres. PL2—4D 12
Wordsworth Rd. PL2—4C 12
Wren Gdns. PL7—5C 16
Wren Ga. PL12—1B 10
Wright Clo. PL1—2C 20
Wycliffe Rd. PL3—1D 22
Wye Gdns. PL3—4F 15
Wykeham Dri. PL2—4D 12
Wyndham La. PL1—3F 21
Wyndham Sq. PL1—3F 21
Wyndham St. E. PL1—3G 21
Wyndham St. W. PL1—3F 21
Wyoming Clo. PL3—5G 15
Wythburn Cres. PL6—6F 7

Yardley Gdns. PL6—6G 7
Yarrow Mead. PL9—6D 24
Yealmpstone Clo. PL7—1G 25
Yealmpstone Dri. PL7—2H 25
Yeats Clo. PL5—1G 13
Yellow Tor Ct. PL12—1C 10
Yellow Tor Rd. PL12—6B 2
Yelverton Clo. PL5—6C 4
Yeo Clo. PL3—6D 14
Yeomans Way. PL7—2G 25
Yewdale Gdns. PL6—6F 7
Yonder St. PL9—1D 26
York Pl. PL2—1D 20
York Rd. PL5—3C 12
York Rd. PL11—2H 19
York St. PL1—3C 20
York Ter. PL2—6D 12

Zion St. PL1—4H 21